Reading
Activities
for Child
Involvement

Reading Activities for Child Involvement

second edition

EVELYN B. SPACHE

Allyn and Bacon, Inc.
Boston   London   Sydney

LIBRARY OF CONGRESS CATALOGING IN PUBLICATION DATA

Spache, Evelyn B.
   Reading activities for child involvement.

   Includes index.
   1. Reading—Handbooks, manuals, etc.   I.   Title.
LB1050.S596   1976   372.4   75–32427

ISBN 0–205–05477–3
ISBN 0–205–04840–4 pbk.

Contents

5 **LANGUAGE DEVELOPMENT AND VOCABULARY**   **126**

8 ADVANCED READING SKILLS   194

9 EXTRA ADDED ATTRACTIONS 224

Preface

The uniqueness of this collection of 472 activities to reinforce reading skills lies in the rationale sections that introduce each skill area. The rationale sections explain: 1) why a skill should be reinforced, 2) how to understand a skill, and 3) what a child should be able to do after completing the activities. Approximately thirty percent of the activities are new to the second edition.

The Cross-Index enables users to find quickly all activities that relate to a particular skill area.

There is no valid reason for our children to learn reading skills through the "3D" method (Dull-Dry-Drill). Reading can be—and should be—stimulating and interesting.

The assistance of the many teachers in Jacksonville, Florida, in testing the activities in their classrooms and in furnishing the author with numerous activities, as well as teacher and child reactions, is greatly appreciated.

I am deeply grateful to my husband, Dr. George D. Spache, Professor Emeritus, University of Florida, for his support and assistance. Also, appreciation is extended to Joann Lowe and Virginia Bispham for their help in organizing material and in suggesting illustrations.

Introduction

Teaching a skill or concept by means of a directed lesson is merely a preliminary step to the actual learning of the skill or concept by the child. Learning takes place *only* when the student reinforces this skill by using it in interesting, meaningful situations. Unless the directed lesson is followed by this reinforcement, future use of the skill may not be realized.

Basic reading teacher's manuals offer excellent guides to teaching skills, but teachers often want follow-up ideas and activities to ensure learning. The activities offered here are specifically designed to reinforce the basic reading skills of any reading program. They were carefully chosen for (1) child interest, (2) availability of materials, (3) ease of directions, (4) variety, and (5) depth of thinking involved.

The same philosophy of meeting individual differences that is evident in *Reading in the Elementary School*, third edition, by Spache and Spache (Allyn and Bacon, 1973), is present throughout these activities. The arrangement is such that the activities correlate with the concepts developed in the textbook. However, the activities are relevant, of course, to any reading program.

WHAT THIS BOOK CONTAINS

Organization. Each new skill area is prefaced by a "Rationale." The rationale explains why the teaching or skill reinforcement should be developed. The teacher should have a clear concept of why the skill is stressed (or not stressed) and how it is to be put to use.

The next section, "The Child Will Learn," is comprised of behavioral outcomes that are consistent with the concept that what is learned should be evident to the learner and readily observable by the teacher. Thus, the behavioral outcomes describe what the child can consciously do and what the teacher can watch him do.

Interspersed with the activities are numerous "Hints" to the teacher. These are ideas that teachers have found useful in any approach to reading. Many have been offered by our fellow teachers.

The activities are purposely not labeled by grade or age level. We feel that many activities for primary children can also be useful for intermediate students reading at much lower levels. Likewise, many advanced reading skills can be emphasized at primary levels. Therefore, activities within each skill area are arranged according to difficulty, from simple to sophisticated. In some instances, only a few changes in words or directions are necessary to make the exercise easier or more challenging, as the teacher desires.

Use of Materials. Throughout this book we have specified use of overhead projectors, chalkboard, charts, films, and particularly acetate folders and markers. When one of these aids is not available, we assume the teacher will use another means of presentation.

We have positive feelings concerning the acetate folders (page protectors). They allow the teacher to use printed or duplicated material again and again, without rewriting on the board or duplicating on paper. Your time and energies are important, and should be conserved wisely in this fashion. There is a second justification for acetate folders. School should be a place where children can make mistakes comfortably. Using the suggested acetate folders (see Teacher-Made Kits), the student can wipe away errors and make a fresh start, with ease and without embarrassment. This is a tremendous aid in building positive self-concepts.

A real attempt has been made to give clear directions for constructing games and activities. The suggested materials are usually available (often free) from school supplies or from local businesses, such as printers, milk companies, or construction companies.

We urge that children construct the games whenever possible. This in itself is functional practice in following directions and in visual-motor coordination.

HOW TO USE THIS BOOK

1. *Try to become familiar with all the activities. Make notes in the margins, underline, and star ideas you think particularly useful.*

2. *Observe your students carefully as they work to diagnose or detect their weaknesses in skill development.*

3. *Prescribe activities to fit needs. Use the cross-index at the back of this book for variety and depth in skill development exercises.*

4. *Be sure the child is aware of his need and knows how an activity or game will help him*

improve. The behavioral outcomes will help both you and the pupil judge his progress.

5. *Do not hesitate to put this book in the children's hands. Many intermediate students are capable of reading and following the directions by themselves. Instructing others in the procedures of play helps to develop leadership ability.*

6. *Titles of chapters seldom give a really clear indication of the contents. For example, Chapter 2, "Early Reading—Related Skills," contains many helpful suggestions for intermediate level students. Chapter 8, "Advanced Reading Skills," has many activities to benefit primary level readers.*

7. *Learning stations have become part of many classroom programs. You will find hundreds of the activities in this book that will add excitement to these stations. Much of teachers' planning time can be eliminated with these readymade activities.*

Teacher-Made Reading Kits

Rationale

In order to meet individual differences in skill development, the teacher must have available materials on many levels and covering a wide variety of skills. The teacher-made kit is a most valuable asset to beginning teachers. Equipped with a skill box, the teacher can begin meeting individual needs immediately, even if school supplies are late or, as is often the case, if they do not meet the pupils' needs.

Teacher-made kits are, naturally, less expensive than commercial kits. They can be made to fill particular needs and can be expanded as needed.

Of all materials used in schools, workbooks are probably the most misused. The inexperienced teacher may order a particular skill book and expect all students to work through it simultaneously, regardless of the child's reading level or particular skill needs. The teacher-made kit makes use of the best of these workbooks in a manner that puts them in the hands of the student who most needs that material.

*   Parents often must pay for student workbooks. If every page is not used and carefully corrected, they feel they have not received their money's worth. Using workbooks to form kits eliminates this problem.*

WHAT KIND OF KIT?

Word attack? Comprehension? Vocabulary? Or fun and games? Many teachers feel insecure in teaching word attack skills. Their college courses may have been particularly weak in this area. Therefore, these teachers would probably feel more secure in beginning with a word attack kit and developing additional kits as needed.

Other teachers, secure in this area, may need kits in different areas because of particular strengths or weaknesses, availability of materials, or student needs.

SELECTION OF WORKSHEETS

We strongly suggest these steps in the selection of materials:

1. *Purchase several workbooks or sets of spirit masters emphasizing one major skill area, each at a different grade level.*

2. *Select worksheets that give a clear indication of the nature of each skill at the top of each page.*

3. *Choose worksheets which offer only one major skill per page.*

4. Try to secure worksheets that give simple and obvious directions at the top of each page.

5. Purchase the teacher's edition of the chosen worksheets for easy correction of errors.

SUPPLIES NEEDED TO ASSEMBLE KIT:

two copies of a student workbook

one copy of teacher's edition for self-correction

8½ × 11 pieces of cardboard* or oaktag (shirt cardboard from a laundry is perfect!)

acetate folders or materials for laminating with drymount press

masking tape

colored mystic tape

wax base markers (crayons or grease pencils)

water-soluble markers (pens or pencils)

attractively decorated box

DIRECTIONS FOR ASSEMBLY

1. Remove staples from each workbook.

2. Cut each workbook down center back.

3. Separate pages of both workbooks into different piles for each skill.

4. Place odd-numbered pages from one workbook on one side of the tagboard, and even-numbered pages from second workbook on reverse side.

5. Seal each page to board all around the edges with masking tape.

---

* Note: 9 × 12 cardboard may be used if you laminate. If using acetate folders, this size would be too large.

COLOR CODING

1. *Choose a different color for each skill. Draw
   solid line of color with a magic marker across
   the top of each page. Mystic tape may be
   used if preferred. If tape is used, overlap it to
   other side, coding both sides at once.
   Suggested code for skills:*

Red		initial consonants
Red · · ·	(red dots)	final and medial consonants
Orange		consonant blends and digraphs
Yellow		short vowels
Green		long vowels
Blue		vowel digraphs and diphthongs
Purple		structural analysis
Brown		alphabetical order
Black		other skills (compounds, contractions, opposites)

2. *Choose a different color for each LEVEL.*

3. *Mark the corner of the sheet with the chosen
   color to indicate level of difficulty. Each
   sheet is now coded with two colors: one for
   SKILL, another for LEVEL.*

4. *Suggested color code for levels:*

   Primer   black

   1   red

   2   orange

   3   yellow

   4   green

5	purple
Jr. Hi	brown
Sr. Hi	black

5. *Place these completed sheets in acetate page protectors. If these are not available, single acetates (transparencies) may be clipped on when needed. (You may want to place Scotch tape across the bottom to prevent the sheet from sliding out.) An alternate method is to run the entire sheet through laminating process.*

6. *File sheets in prepared box, grouping skill-coded sheets by sections.*

7. *Place teachers' editions in rear of box.*

SKILL BOX

1. *Choose any carton that will hold the sheets upright for easy viewing.*

2. *Cut down one side for easy removal and refiling of sheets.*

3. *Cover box with contact paper or with enamel paint.*

4. *Place card with skill code on front or side of box to assist students in refiling sheets.*

VARIATIONS

Kits may be made for many types of activities. Comprehension kits are popular, using an arrangement similar to that in the illustration.

red	Sequence
orange	Context clues
yellow	Main idea

blue   Getting facts

purple   Following directions

black   Dictionary skills, etc.

Vocabulary kits, *using crossword and other paper and pencil puzzles, are excellent. Coding is not necessary for these kits but will be helpful if several levels of difficulty are included. Be sure to have answer keys available for self-correction.*

TIPS

1. *The simplest arrangement is merely to place the worksheets in the acetate envelope and file it. However, these sheets lack body and will not stand up in the file box. Also, they are more inclined to slide off desks onto the floor and become scratched.*

2. *Choose marking pens with care! When shopping, take along an acetate to try various brands of markers. Make sure they have water soluble ink and fine tips. See that they do not "bead" but make clear, firm lines. Check to see that a piece of dampened sponge, a soft cloth, or Nu-Von will easily remove marks.*

ILLUSTRATION. SKILL BOX.

3. *Wax or plastic base markers:* (a) *Grease pencils are usable but a point is difficult to maintain. Also, primary children are apt to unravel them.* (b) *Crayons work well, but you will need small pencil sharpeners to keep a good point.* (c) *Plastic markers are excellent. All of these are easily erased with dry Nu-Von or a facial tissue.* (d) *Transparency pencils of some types often give excellent results.*

4. *A smaller, matching box may be placed in the front of the kit to hold marking materials.*

CONCLUSION

Kits can be made from various materials for a multiplicity of purposes. Your creative ideas alone set the limits. The basic purpose is to give students the proper skill sheets *when* they *need* them.

SUGGESTED MATERIALS FOR KITS

PAGE PROTECTORS

We have had reports of excellent service from

Transparent Industrial Envelope, Inc.
386 Park Avenue South
New York, New York 10016
(order Stock #T11–75).

Many workbooks that accompany basal readers can be adapted to kits, providing they do not depend on use of the textbook for reference.

PERCEPTUAL KIT

> *Continental Press, Inc., Elizabethtown,
> Pennsylvania 17022:* Visual Readiness
> Skills, *levels 1 and 2;* Seeing Likenesses and
> Differences, *levels 1, 2, and 3;* Visual-Motor
> Skills, *levels 1 and 2* (*spirit masters*).

> *Milliken Publishing Company, 611 Olive Street,
> St. Louis, Missouri 63101:* Visual Discrimi-
> nation; Motor and Hand-Eye Coordination
> (*spirit masters*).

WORD RECOGNITION AND
VOCABULARY

> *Continental Press, Inc., Elizabethtown,
> Pennsylvania 17022:* Crossword Puzzles,
> *levels 1 through 6* (*spirit masters*).

> *Garrard Publishing Company, 1607 North Market
> Street, Champaign, Illinois 61820:* Dolch
> Puzzle Book, *I* (easy) *and II* (harder).

> *IMED Publishers, 1415 Westwood Boulevard, Los
> Angeles, California 90024:* Crossword
> Puzzles for Word Power—*Starter Books 1
> and 2; Books 1 through 3.*

> *Grosset and Dunlap, Inc., Treasure Books
> Division, 51 Madison Avenue, New York,
> New York 10010: Crossword Puzzle Series—*
> Crossword Puzzles, *grades 2 through 6;*
> Famous People, *grades 5 and 6;* Animal
> Crossword Puzzles, *grades 4 and 5;* Old
> Testament, *grades 4 and 5;* New Testament,
> *grades 4 and 5;* Fairy Tales, *grades 3 and 4;*
> Sports Heroes, *grades 4 and 5;* Great
> Americans, *grades 4 and 5;* Great
> Inventions, *grades 4 and 5*

> Scholastic Book Services, *904 Sylvan Avenue,
> Englewood Cliffs, New Jersey:* Scope: *Word
> skills, levels 1 and 2* (*intended for inter-
> mediate and above*).

WORD ANALYSIS

*American Education Publications, Education
Center, Columbus, Ohio 43216:* Phonics
and Word Power, *programs 1 through 3.*

*American Book Company, 55 Fifth Avenue, New
York, New York 10003:* READ Series Skill
Books, *levels 1 through 6.*

*Educator's Publishing Service, Inc., 75 Moulton
Street, Cambridge, Massachusetts 02138:*
Primary Phonics, *Workbook 1, and other
phonics.*

*Ginn and Company, a Xerox Education
Company, 191 Spring Street, Lexington,
Massachusetts 02173:* Ginn Word
Enrichment Program—Consonant Sounds
and Symbols; Vowels and Variants; Sounds
and Syllables; More Sounds and Syllables;
Working with Words.

*Lyons and Carnahan, Educational Division of
Meredith Corporation, 407 East 25th Street,
Chicago, Illinois 60616:* Phonics We Use,
primer to grade 6 (Books A–G).

*McCormick-Mathers Publishing Company,
Division of Litton Educational Publishing,
450 West 53rd Street, New York, New York
10001:* Speedboat, *and others, levels 1
through 6.*

*Charles E. Merrill Publishing Company, 1300
Alum Creek Drive, Columbus, Ohio 43216:*
Phonics Skills, *Textbooks A through D.*

*Milliken Publishing Company, 611 Olive Street,
St. Louis, Missouri 63101:* Phonics, *grades
1 through 3 (spirit masters).*

*Modern Curriculum Press, 13900 Prospect Road,
Cleveland, Ohio 44136:* Phonics Is Fun,
Readiness Books 1 and 2; Phonics
Workbooks, *grades 1 through 3.*

COMPREHENSION AND STUDY SKILLS

Allyn and Bacon, Inc., 470 Atlantic Avenue, Boston, Massachusetts 02210: Sheldon Series—Activity Books, *grades 4 through 6 (especially strong in study and location skills, graphs, maps).*

American Education Publications, Education Center, Columbus, Ohio 43216: My Weekly Reader *Practice Books*—Map Skills, *grades 2 through 6;* Science Reading Adventures, *grades 1 through 6;* Read-Study-Think, *grades 1 through 6.*

Barnell-Loft, Ltd., 111 South Centre Avenue, Rockville Centre, Long Island, New York 11470: Specific Skill Series, grades 1 through 6—Using the Context; Working with Sounds; Getting the Facts; Locating the Answer; Following Directions.

Continental Press, Inc., Elizabethtown, Pennsylvania 17022: Reading-Thinking Skills, *grades 1 through 6 (spirit masters).*

Follett Publishing Company, 1010 West Washington Boulevard, Chicago, Illinois 60607: Turner Livingston Reading Series *(double pages, so you must use both sides of page protectors).*

J. B. Lippincott Company, East Washington Square, Philadelphia, Pennsylvania 19105: Reading for Meaning Workbooks, *grades 4 through 6.*

Charles E. Merrill Publishing Company, 1300 Alum Creek Drive, Columbus, Ohio 43216: Diagnostic Reading Workbooks, *grades 1 through 6*—Nip the Bear, *grade 1;* Red Deer, Indian Boy, *grade 2;* Scottie and His Friends, *grade 3;* Adventure Trails, *grade 4;* Exploring Today, *grade 5;* Looking Ahead, *grade 6. Merrill,* Reading Skill Texts, *grades 1 through 6*—Bibs, *grade 1;* Nicky, *grade 2;* Uncle Funny Bunny, *grade 3;*

Uncle Ben, *grade 4;* Tom Trott, *grade 5;*
Pat the Pilot, *grade 6.*

*Milliken Publishing Company, 611 Olive Street,
St. Louis, Missouri 63101:* Reading Series
(*spirit masters*).

*Prentice-Hall, Inc., Englewood Cliffs, New Jersey
07632:* Be a Better Reader, *Foundations
Books A, B, and C.*

*Reader's Digest Services, Inc., Educational
Division, Pleasantville, New York 10570:*
Reading Skill Builders and Practice Pads,
grades 1 through 6.

*Science Research Associates, 259 East Erie Street,
Chicago, Illinois 60611:* The Job Ahead
Series (*career education for teenagers*).

*Visual Materials, Inc., 2549 Middlefield Road,
Redwood City, California 94603: A large
variety of spirit masters (send for
descriptions*).

*Webster Division, McGraw-Hill Book Company,
Manchester Road, Manchester, Missouri
63011:* New Practice Readers,
grades 2 through 6—Books A, B, C; 1, 2, 3.

2

Prereading
Skills

I. VISUAL SKILLS

Rationale

> About half the children who enter the first grade can-
> not control their eyes well enough to follow a line of
> objects or printed words. They do not have enough
> two-eyed coordination (binocular control) to look
> sequentially along a line of images. One or both eyes
> tend to wander away from the pictures or words the
> child is trying to look at. Yet the reading act demands
> a high degree of binocular control in maintaining
> attention on a line from left to right. Without good
> binocular coordination, even keeping one's place on
> the line is difficult, not to mention learning to read
> accurately.

THE CHILD WILL LEARN:

to maintain fixation on a moving object
to follow a moving object with his eyes
to move easily from point to point with his eyes
to maintain stable fixation on a moving object
    while he is moving
to maintain sequential fixation on a line of objects
to practice skills related to visual memory

BINOCULAR SKILLS

1. Walking beam.* Directions for constructing beam: The only material needed is a standard 2 × 4 about twelve to fourteen feet in length. Cut three eighteen-inch pieces from the board. These pieces will be the braces. The remaining footage (approximately eight to ten feet) will be the walking beam. Using a saw, cut notches in each of three braces, as shown in Illustration 1(a). Place beam in four-inch notch for beginners. This is an inexpensive and useful piece of equipment.

General instructions: Have a fixation target, such as X on the blackboard or a small picture about eighteen to twenty inches below eye level opposite the end of the beam. Children should always look at this target when exercising on the beam. Keep a record to indicate when pupils can perform these tasks.

Indian walk. Have children walk Indian fashion, heel touching toe, along the beam. Keep eyes fixed on the target.

Butterfly. Using the Indian walk, spread arms out like a butterfly, moving them up and down slowly, while moving along the beam.

---

* Adapted from G. N. Getman, *How To Develop Your Child's Intelligence* (Irvine, Calif.: Research Publications). By permission.

Backward walk.   Walk backwards on the beam, toe and heel fashion. Keep eyes on the target.

Backward butterfly.   Walk backwards on the beam, moving arms up and down slowly like a butterfly.

Forward and backward.   Walk forward until teacher or other pupil says "Stop," then reverse, moving backward. Use Indian walk, heel to toe, in each direction.

Learning distances.   Put a red stripe across the beam at the middle, and put green stripes at the one-quarter and three-quarter points. Use the forward and backward movements upon command, using the words "one-half," "one-quarter," "two-quarters," or "three-quarters."

Peripheral targets.   Place the walking beam parallel to the wall or chalkboard. Position the beam about two feet from the wall. Put a red circle at the child's eye level, on the wall or board at a point opposite the halfway mark on the beam. Have children try to walk the beam without looking at that point, with arms extended to the side, until they think they are even with the red circle and can touch it. Repeat exercise with beam placed at an angle (forty-five degrees or less) to the wall. Again, have them try to touch the red circle without looking at it. Practice touching the side targets while walking backwards, while walking forward, and starting from either end of the beam.

ILLUSTRATION 1 (A). BRACE FOR WALKING BEAM.

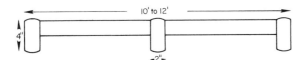

ILLUSTRATION 1 (B). SIDE VIEW OF WALKING BEAM.

OCULAR MOTILITY

2. This activity is helpful to relieve visual tension from doing close work. Place four large cards, with one numeral on each card (1, 2, 3, 4), on the four walls (near the corners) of the side of the room the children are facing. Two cards will be high, near the ceiling; two low, near the floor. Place the cards as near the corners as possible. Each child has an index card or folded sheet of paper. He places this edgewise to his nose so he

Walking Beam

| Name | 4″ Beam | | | | | | | 2″ Beam | | | | | | |
	Indian	Butterfly	Backward	Backward Butterfly	Forward & Backward	Distances	Targets	Indian	Butterfly	Backward	Backward Butterfly	Forward & Backward	Distances	Targets

ILLUSTRATION 1 (C).

can see two of the numbers with one eye, the other half of the room with the other eye (he may close one eye at a time to check this). With both eyes open, he looks at the numbers the teacher (or leader) calls, such as "1, 3, 4, 2, 3, 1, 4, 3."

This activity causes the student to use both eyes independently at far point, relieving tiredness from working at desk level.

3.   Suspend a small rubber ball (or any similar object) at the child's eye level from a doorway, from a light fixture, or from your hand. Gently swing the ball to and fro, in a circle, and from side to side, a foot or two from his face, while he follows it with his eyes. To vary this exercise, hang the ball about three feet from the floor, and have the child watch it while lying directly beneath it. Or have the child try to follow the ball's movement with a jar four or five inches in diameter, without hitting sides of jar. This can be varied by asking the child to touch the ball in flight with his forefinger, from beneath the ball or from the side.

VISUAL MEMORY

4.   Slowly print a word, a group of letters, or numbers on the board. Then, as a small group of children cover (or close) their eyes, erase one figure or letter. Students use their visual memory to recall what is missing. Later, two or more letters may be eliminated.

VARIATION

> *Hold up a drawing or picture. Then cover part of it with a card. Children tell what has been covered.*

5.   Three children stand in front of the class. The class notes their clothing—Sally's bow, Fred's untied shoe, and so on. The three children leave the room and one child changes something about his or her appearance before returning. Their class-mates notice what was changed.

      6. To check visual memory, have children look at the back of the room, then ask them these questions:

      1.   What is on top of the bookcase?

      2.   Name the color of the flower vase.

      3.   What is in the center of the library table?

Use additional questions that apply to your classroom.

      7. While students are out of the room, change several items around so they can observe what has been altered.

EXAMPLES

cover the aquarium
change the reading circle
change months on the calendar
hang a new picture
move the mirror

      8. Make twenty slits in a large piece of oaktag, so that cards 3 × 4 inches can be inserted by paper clips. Print a word or letter on ten of the cards, and make a duplicate card for each one. Number the cards on the back from one to ten (making two of each number). Place the cards on the board, with the words or letters facing the children. The children are divided into two equal teams. The first child from one team comes up to the front and must say the word or sound and find its mate before he turns the card over to see if the numbers match. If they do match, they remain turned so the numbers show, and his team is given one point. If they do not match, the cards are turned back so the words or letters are showing. Then a member of the opposing team is given a chance to match two numbers by calling out and turning two other cards. The game continues until all cards have been matched, and the team with the most points wins the game.

9. Make about ten flash cards using written nouns the group has studied. Be sure all the words are nouns which can be illustrated. Show the group the flash cards, one after the other, fairly quickly.

After all cards have been shown, allow the group fifteen minutes to illustrate as many words as they can remember. Do *not* evaluate art skill in this activity. The object is to stimulate *visual memory*.

During the game the board may look like this.

chop	dog	4	8
3	friend	3	chop
ate	since	I	this
since	8	this	friend
4	ate	I	dog

ILLUSTRATION 8.

Leave cards available so individuals can check their own memories.

EXAMPLE

man	dog	jar	bottle
bus	ring	apple	jumprope

VARIATION

> *Make a transparency with all of the words you plan to use. Show them on the overhead projector just long enough for all students to read all the words. (Don't allow them to write the words!)*
>
> *Increase or decrease the number of words according to the level of the group participating.*

II. VISUAL-MOTOR SKILLS

Rationale

> *Discrimination of the forms and shapes that constitute letters is based fundamentally on the bodily hand and eye experiences of the child. Up-down, front-back, near-far, and left-right discriminations are first learned in the muscles. Gradually, during the early years of life, the child learns to translate the muscular cues of distance, size, directionality, and shape into visual cues. He moves slowly from the circle to the cross, the straight line, the square, the diagonal line, the diamond, and other cues to size, directionality, and the like. Only when this development is far advanced is the child ready to apply these visual cues in the act of reading. Many primary children have not reached this stage of development, as shown in their difficulties in reproducing forms, matching forms, attempting to draw common objects, and trying to write letters.*

Children vary considerably in their needs for these training exercises. Some well developed, highly coordinated children may be able to move through the exercises in a week or two. Other children need much longer periods, perhaps extending to months, before they achieve rapid, fluent hand-eye coordination and are really ready for success in reading.

Some children will be admitted to the basal reading program on the basis of their readiness test scores. Yet they may still need this basic visual training for some time afterward. It is expected that teachers will continue to offer this training to children until their chalkboard and near-point performances show that it is no longer needed.

THE CHILD WILL LEARN:

to hold fixation while executing a variety of
  bodily movements
to execute directionality in coordinated
  hand-eye movements
to achieve rhythmic hand-eye movements
to recognize and execute common shapes by
  exercises with geometric forms
to make discriminations involving directionality,
  size, shape, distance, etc.

BODILY COORDINATION*

10. The balance disc provides an independent activity for bodily coordination. The child maintains balance while

---

* Also see Activity 1, walking beam.

(a) moving feet from center to outside edges of disc, (b) raising one foot at a time, and (c) bending his knees, turning around, or executing other movements.

The disc should be painted with a rough texture paint (add coarse sand), or use nonslip rubber strips such as in bathtubs. You may wish to use the disc on a carpeted area or on heavy cardboard so as to keep corners from bumping the floor.

Materials: a square or round piece of five-eighths-inch plywood, approximately eighteen inches in diameter; one 2 × 4 × 4 piece of wood, epoxy, bolt and nut (about two and one-half inches).

Directions: With epoxy, glue the 2 × 4 block flat to the underside of plywood. Put a bolt through block and plywood, and secure the bolt on top. File off any excess part of bolt. Place nonslip strips on top surface. This is simple to construct and costs less than one dollar for a wonderful piece of balance equipment.

VARIATION

> For students who are ready for further balance skills, add an additional 2 × 4 block to the underside. This is great fun.

11. Make a likeness of a seven-foot ladder on the floor with masking tape. Some of the activities you can do are:

Hop on right foot in each space, then on left foot.

Hop with both feet.

Duck walk.

Walk with one foot on each side of the frame.

Walk the frame on all fours.

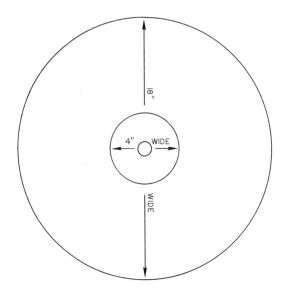

ILLUSTRATION 10. BALANCE DISC.

12. Activities with a long jumprope, placed on the floor:

> With alternate feet, jump from side to side.
>
> Jump from side to side with both feet.
>
> Jump on one foot from side to side.
>
> Walk the rope.
>
> Walk on all fours, straddling the rope.
>
> Duck walk, straddling the rope.

DIRECTIONALITY

13. Each child holds a ball, eraser, or other easy-to-hold object. Directions are given orally for them to hold the object in the position asked for.

over *your head.*
under *your chin.*
behind *your back.*
between *your knees.*

14. Place a sturdy table and chair before the group. One child places himself in various positions (*under* the table, *on* the chair, *beside* the chair, and so on). Children in group describe the action. They take turns being the "demonstrator."

15. Project a picture on the screen (or have students study a picture in the text), directing the class to note the locations of objects and people. Then remove the picture and encourage students to describe the place, relationship of the people, or the things with such words as "below," "next to," or "above."

CHALKBOARD ACTIVITIES*

General instructions: All chalkboard work is done with the child standing at a comfortable writing distance from the chalkboard. Center the chalkboard at the level of the child's nose. There is usually no problem of maintaining motivation, since the teacher must work right with the child. If a child finds some particular procedure too difficult for him, drop back to a simpler procedure. The basic rule is *never to advance the child too rapidly.* Give him a rest period if he exhibits motor fatigue. Training periods should not be longer than ten to fifteen minutes a day, but should occur daily.
Use a felt-tip marking pen to make patterns on chalkboard. These may be removed later with alcohol.

---

* Adapted from work done by Dr. Leo Manas, who has used them extensively in his optometric practice.

16.   Unimanual Training Procedures.

A.   Make a vertical row of dots on the chalkboard, about ten inches to the right of the center position, and a similar row of dots to the left of center. Label each dot on the same horizontal line similarly; the vertical spacing between the dots should be about three inches. The pattern will look like this:

A •   • A

B •   • B

C •   • C

The child scribes from left to right in an unbroken line, joining the dots.

B.   In the variation below, the child scribes from left to right, upward. The child must make a continuous line starting from one dot and ending at the other dot before we consider that he has developed adequate performance ability.

C.   Combining straight and oblique lines. Using the rows of dots, ask the child to draw both horizontally (as in A) and obliquely, from the dot at the right to the second dot at the left:

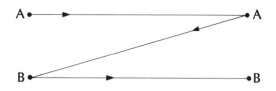

D. Repeat, using the vertical spacing of dots and the oblique spacing, as in B:

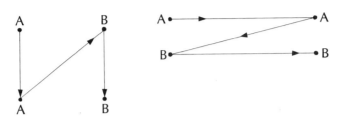

The child should make a continuous, rapid line from each dot to the next. *Note:* These lines are drawn straight, quickly, and with a single free motion, *not* painstakingly slowly with only one hand or wrist movement.

When the child can perform these visual-kinesthetic procedures with ease and accuracy, we proceed to "Chase the leader."

17. "Chase the leader." Construct a series of three or more dots on a chalkboard, and label them A, B, C, and so on. The child must go in the proper direction and continuously scribe a line from A to B and on to the last letter on the chalkboard. This teaches recognition of the letters of the alphabet in proper sequence and develops ability to scribe lines rapidly in all directions; it teaches the child to make a rapid shift in direction (to draw angles) and develops his ability to stay on his primary target in spite of the distraction of other lines in the

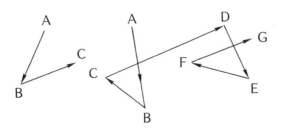

ILLUSTRATION 17.

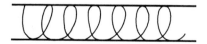

ILLUSTRATION 18 (A).

field of view. Start with three dots, then increase to five, seven, or more.

18.   Repetitive forms. This technique develops rhythm, shape, or form, and the ability to maintain constancy of size. Two parallel lines about six inches apart are constructed across the board, at the nose level of the child. He starts with his chalk about four inches from the left edge of the lines and makes circles in a counterclockwise direction, moving slowly toward the right as he scribes his circles. It looks like Illustration 18(a). As a variation of this, have the child scribe vertical lines in the same manner, as in Illustration 18 (b). These lines may be used later for practice in letter formation and spacing.

BIMANUAL TRAINING PROCEDURES

19.   Bimanual circles. A fixation point (an X) is placed on the chalkboard at the nose level of the child. The child stands about ten inches from the chalkboard. He holds a piece of chalk in each hand and places the chalk in contact with the board at about one inch from the fixation point. The left chalk is one inch to the left of the fixation point, and the right chalk one inch to its right. The child starts upward with each hand, making a circle pattern on the board with each hand simultaneously. The left hand is moving counterclockwise and the right hand clockwise.

ILLUSTRATION 18 (B).

ILLUSTRATION 19.

The child continues making the circles with both hands, trying to improve on the contour of the form to make a perfect circle.

These movements may be changed by having the left hand move clockwise and the right counterclockwise, or by having both hands moving in the same direction. Whenever the board gets filled with circles, it is erased and a new fixation point is marked. The child then continues the bimanual procedures.

20. Bimanual straight lines. The teacher places a large circle of dots on the chalkboard or easel, with a large center dot at the height of the child's eyes. The dots around the circle are lettered or numbered; if the child cannot read these symbols, the teacher indicates the two dots for the starting points. The child then tries to draw with both hands, from two dots on opposite edges of the circle to the center dot, or the reverse, from the center to two opposite outer dots. Extend this training so that the child can draw simultaneously from any two dots to the center or the reverse. The lines should be drawn at once, straight and quickly, once the starting points have been identified. Dots scattered in any order on the blackboard, to be connected with straight lines, is a sound, unimanual extension of this type of exercise.

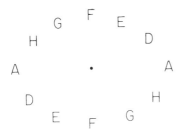

ILLUSTRATION 20.

When all the chalkboard exercises have been completed satisfactorily, you may wish to repeat exercises on paper at the child's desk. The chalkboard training should make the child progress somewhat faster in the desk exercises. This near-point training can go on simultaneously with other desk activities, such as the Continental Press worksheets.

21. Template training.* The templates are geometric forms cut out of 9 × 12 masonite boards or heavy cardboard. The cutout portion is about seven inches tall, off center, so that the child can hold onto the board comfortably with the non-writing hand. Forms include the circle, square, triangle, rectangle, and diamond. Templates containing smaller forms, all five, may be constructed for use at the desk.

Directions:

1. *Child holds template against chalkboard with one hand, centered a little below his nose. He stands erect, about twelve to fifteen inches from the board.*

2. *With the chalk, the child traces clockwise inside the cutout, keeping the chalk against the edge. He scribes around and around, starting always at the top, while he or the teacher counts (to two for the circle, to three or four for the other forms). Note: If the inside edges of the template are rough, bind the edges with mystic tape to provide a smoother surface.*

3. *Continue until child can trace the shape freely without breaks or deviations from the edge. Then repeat entire procedure in counter-clockwise direction.*

4. *When performance becomes smooth, let child try the shape with writing hand without aid of template.*

---

* Adapted from the suggestions of the *Teacher's Manual for Perceptual Training,* Winter Haven Lions Research Foundation, Box 1045, Winter Haven, Florida.

> 5. *Use desk templates in same fashion, first clockwise, with and without template. When forms are mastered, use different shapes to make designs and pictures.*

22. *Hint:* Children who have difficulty writing may need small muscle activities. Have several objects that require finger-thumb pressure, such as clothespins and lines or cardboard with marks showing where to clip. Other activities may include:

> *Squeezing clay.*
>
> *Squeezing a small, soft ball.*
>
> *Making pegboard designs.*
>
> *Pushing in and pulling out thumbtacks or brads.*
>
> *Manipulating small blocks into patterns.*

23. A small group of children form a circle, one child in the center. The center child tosses a beanbag to another child. If he catches it, he tosses it back to the center child; if missed, they exchange places.

24. Instructional aid: On shirt cardboard or other stiff paper, paint or color a large, simple design. With a hole-puncher, perforate around the design. Children develop visual-motor skills by outlining the design with yarn and a blunt needle or with long bootlaces. A child must unlace a card before returning it to the box. To prevent tangling, laces may be kept stuck into a sponge on a shelf.

25. Two teams are formed, and each lines up so the first child in each line is several feet from a trash can. Each child has a turn to toss a bean bag (eraser, sponge) into the container.

Each team has a "retriever" who tosses the object to the next person in line. This is an excellent rainy day activity.

26. Suspend a small rubber ball (three to four inches in diameter) from a rod (a chart rack is good), so that it hangs at about the children's chest level. Two players bunt the ball back and forth to each other, using rolling pins—the wooden kitchen variety is best. To suspend the ball, staple a cord or yarn to the ball and hang it from the rod.

27. Cut the top and one side (just above the handle) from a large plastic bleach bottle. Use this for a mitt. Form a circle, with one child in the middle. Each child must have a mitt. Give the child in the center a small whiffle ball or a small bean-bag. The center child tosses the beanbag from his mitt to a child in the circle. That child catches it in his mitt and tosses it back to the center.

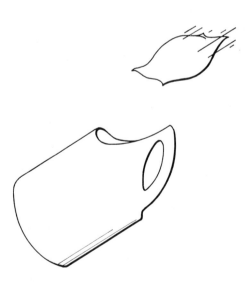

ILLUSTRATION 27.

28. Children can make their own jigsaw puzzles. Each child brings in a colorful picture from a magazine or discarded storybook. The picture is pasted on light cardboard. With pencil or crayon, draw odd-shaped lines to become puzzle pieces. Students cut these apart with strong scissors. Number each piece of the puzzle with the same number so that the puzzles will not become mixed. Place each puzzle in a separate manila envelope for placement in a puzzle file. Number the envelope the same number as the puzzle pieces.

III. VISUAL DISCRIMINATION SKILLS

Rationale

Progress in the continuum from muscular learning to visual learning means moving toward the fine discriminations demanded by letters and words. This ability to read and write the symbols of language we call visual discrimination. *Developmental stages include, first, form discrimination, then three-dimensional materials, and, later, use of paper and pencil in two-dimensional reproduction and matching. Shapes and forms are thus closely related to the hand-eye movements of writing and the visual movements of reading. Recognition of word shapes proceeds directly from the two- and three-dimensional experiences with other forms and shapes.*

Learning to write strengthens and reinforces the visual act of reading; only occasionally can children learn to read who cannot form letters accurately.

THE CHILD WILL LEARN:

to recognize three-dimensional patterns and
designs.
to reproduce or match two-dimensional objects
or forms.
to recognize word configurations.
to recognize colors and shades of colors.

FORM DISCRIMINATION

29.   On ditto masters draw squares and/or circles,
and run off copies for the children. Instruct the children to draw
in the square or circle something observed in the classroom or
in the community. Each day during the week change the location
for observation, such as outside, in a store, cafeteria, and so on.
At the end of the week the children may share their ideas.

30.   Draw a simple, basic shape on the blackboard
and see how many objects the children can make from it. Sharing
ideas in a brief discussion will stimulate ideas. You can add more
and more shapes. Later, students may draw on paper as many
different objects as they can, using these basic shapes. This can
also be done with letters.

31.   In a discussion of shapes, ask the children to look
around the room or out the window and compare shapes with
a form you are holding (square, circle, and so on).

32.   Use magazines as a source of pictures that contain various fundamental shapes and mount the pictures on oaktag or stiff paper. Have children observe each illustration closely

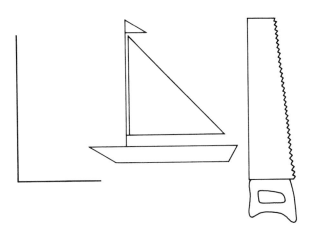

ILLUSTRATION 30.

to see how many different shapes (squares, circles) they can find in each picture. Some children can make a list of items seen.

SHAPE BINGO

√ **33.** Make a set of six to eight Bingo grid cards (see Illustration 33). It should contain four circles, four triangles, four squares, and four diamonds, each outlined in one of four colors —red, blue, green, and yellow.

Make a set of flash cards with one shape on each card. There will be one color each of each shape.

Flash the cards so children get a five-second look at each card. Then they use cut-up markers (about an inch square) to position on their Bingo cards. A *Bingo* wins.*

34. On chalkboard or on a transparency write pairs of words easily confused through spelling reversals, for instance, pan, nap; rat, tar; was, saw; draw, ward. Use one word of each pair in a sentence and have students indicate the one you used.

---

* Suggested by Helen Hanson. By permission.

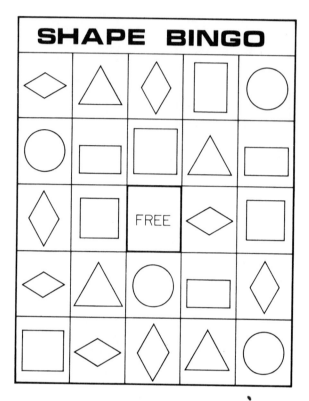

ILLUSTRATION 33.

After noting the similarities in visual detail, discuss the differences in spelling and meaning. Then have students make sentences using both words in each pair.

√ **35.** If you have access to a wallpaper sample book, paste ten different designs on sixty 2 × 3 inch cards, repeating each design six times. Deal fifteen cards each to four players. They hold the cards in their hands.

The first player turns over one card from his hand and places the card in the center. Other players follow, turning their cards over until there is a match. The first person to place a matching card on the table gets all the cards in the center, which he stacks as a "book." If no one has a match, the next player adds a card to the one on the table. The next winner gets all those cards. The player with the most "books" wins.

36. A nature walk may be used to gather objects of different shapes (grass blades, leaves, stones, twigs). Mount the collection on charts and compare the shapes. Pictures may be used to compare objects with similar or different shapes.

37. Common highway warning signs may be made from oaktag. These may be placed face down on a table. Children take turns choosing a sign, reading it to the group, explaining its meaning, and telling where this sign may be found. Signs such as *Stop, Railroad Crossing, Danger,* or *Keep Out* may be used.

LETTER FORMATION

38. Instructional aid: On sheets of oaktag (approximately 5 × 15 inches) write a letter of the alphabet in a bold script. Cover this with an acetate sheet (or laminate it). The child practices the form with a suitable marker. Directional arrows or numbers may be used to aid in proper formation.

39. Children seldom confuse capital B, so this method may help them distinguish lowercase b and d. The lowercase b is just like the capital B without the top curve: B   b.

✓   **40.** Some pupils have a difficult time forming letters. This activity is fun to do, and very helpful. Pupils roll out modeling clay into long strips. They form letters by arranging the clay on top of large letters made by the teacher.

41. Instructional aid: Cut letters from sandpaper or paint a mixture of Elmer's glue and sand over cutout letters. Students trace over a letter with their hands, then try to form it themselves. The rough texture aids in kinesthetic memory. Sand or grain sprinkled on glue works well.

COLOR DISCRIMINATION

42. Hold up a piece of colored construction paper and ask, "If you are wearing something this color, stand up." Other class members observe and name the object worn.

VARIATION

> (a) *A child names an object visible in the room that is the same color as the paper. The game continues until many objects have been named.* (b) *Students think of a fruit, vegetable, or other object of that color.*

43. Cut rectangles (regular playing card size is good) of all the colors being learned. A leader holds two of the cards up for the players to see. Then the leader turns around and adds one more color card to his or her "hand." Players must tell what color has been added. The leader then adds additional cards until all of the colors are added to the "hand." Children may take turns as leader. Use this activity with a small group.

44. *Hint:* Young children may be able to discriminate the difference between red and blue but may not be able to recognize various shades of red as being red (or other color). To aid in recognizing different shades of a color, use a discarded mail-order catalog as a resource. Children work on one color at a time, finding illustrations in as many shades of that color as they can locate. These illustrations may be mounted on a chart labeled "shades of red" or other color.

45. *Hint:* You can get folders from a local paint store that show clear samples of many shades of all colors. These are excellent to post on a bulletin board. The names of the shades are interesting, such as canary yellow, bronze beige, hot pink, soft melon, and so on.

IV. AUDITORY SKILLS

Rationale

The goal of discriminating letter sounds and words is founded on many types of listening exercises. The child must first be able to discriminate pitch, loudness, duration, and rhythmic patterns or sequences of sounds, for these are the auditory cues to letters and words. These auditory skills are also essential to phonic and structural analysis in order to discriminate the pitches of letter sounds and of inflection, the loudness that determines accent, and the comparative duration of the sounds of vowels and consonants. Auditory memory functions in listening to words and syllable sequences.

Listening skills are also closely related to success in reading, for the thinking demanded parallels that used in reading. Listening is not a natural skill that matures with age; it must be trained. One goal of listening training is to help the child do the types of thinking demanded in reading.

A child's ability to think in various ways in listening and reading situations depends directly on the training given by teachers' questions. If questioning is limited to parrotlike recall of details, as is common in our classrooms, children will fail to develop skill in making judgments, inferences, conclusions, interpretations, or evaluations. Listening training is an excellent opportunity to provide practice in these thinking skills, and thus to promote reading developments.

THE CHILD WILL LEARN:

to attend to and distinguish animal and
environmental sounds

to discriminate between loud and soft sounds

to recognize pitch differences in common sounds
and speech sounds

to differentiate sounds of varying duration

to respond to and remember the rhythm of
speech sounds

to recognize and remember sequences of sounds

to follow directions

to anticipate ideas in a context

to retell or interpret continuous material

AUDITORY MEMORY AND DISCRIMINATION

46.   Children pretend they are in a cave where echoes
bounce from wall to wall. The leader of the expedition makes
various sounds, words, sentences. The followers repeat each
one, trying to use the same inflections, pitch, and so forth as an
echo.

47.   *Hint:*   When children are waiting in line (why
waste this time?) try this auditory discrimination, or listening
activity. The teacher says, "Raise your hand if . . ."

your name begins like *Billy.*

you're wearing something green (or other color).

your birthday is in _____ (month).

you got up before 7:00 this morning.

Capable students may form a committee to compile a
list of such questions to be used at a later time of waiting.

48. A game for auditory discrimination and rhythm. Children are given dittoed sheets marked with a large circle in which a path of squares has been drawn (see Illustration 48). Give each child a marker of some sort. The teacher claps two or three times, and children move their markers through the squares according to the number of claps they hear. Children who finish too soon or too slowly need further practice to improve these skills.

49. The children listen while you pronounce several unrelated words, such as "deer, candy, pencil, ring." Students try to remember these words and supply the correct ones when you say "something sweet," "something to wear," "made of wood," "has four legs."

The maturity of the group will determine the complexity of your statements.

50. After discussing different kinds of listening experiences and sounds, have the pupils write a paragraph similar to the one on the top of page 44.

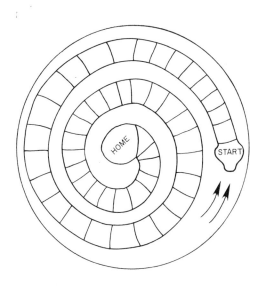

ILLUSTRATION 48.

On my way to school I heard _____.

Yesterday, while I was outside, I heard _____.

In the grocery store I heard _____.

With primary children this activity may be done orally.

51. After reading the book *Loudest Noise in the World* by Benjamin Elkin, discuss noises with children. Discuss sounds they like or sounds they don't like and where they may have heard these sounds.

52. It is fun to tape voices and let members of the group listen to the tape and identify the voices they hear. Or several children may go behind a screen; then one child speaks. The group tries to identify the child's voice.

53. The teacher or leader says words that depict sounds. The student names things that could cause these sounds. The responses may be listed on the board if desired.

EXAMPLES

snap	swoosh	sputter
crunch	fizz	flap
boom	whistle	whine
crackle	scratch	gurgle

VARIATION

Older students can use the above words (and others they think of) as headings. They write under the headings situations in which they might hear these sounds.

54. Supply each student with scissors, an old magazine, and a large sheet of construction paper. At the top of the paper write a large letter in both upper and lower cases, as Cc. Have children clip from the magazines as many pictures of things beginning with hard C as they can find, and paste them under the letter, for example, cow, car, coat, cat.

The class may search for pictures with the same initial sound, or each child may use a different letter and later combine his sheet with those of the other students to form a picture dictionary.

A blend of letters (like *cl*) may be used as a heading but should not be interchanged with other initial sounds; for example, a picture of a cloud should not be used to illustrate the initial sound c.

55. Record a collection of sounds on a tape-recorder. After a small group listens to one sound, take time to discuss what it might be.

EXAMPLES

telephone being dialed	dog barking
busy signal	dog whining
ringing	cat's meow
beep tones of push button phone	bird calls
car starting	ambulance siren
brakes screeching	people clapping

VARIATION

Put the tape on a listening station. Children listen and write their guess about each sound. Have an answer card available, but encourage students to listen several times before checking the answer.

V. TACTILE DISCRIMINATION

Rationale

It has been said that a word is not an island unto itself but is the intersection of a group of ideas or memories. Central to this network is the auditory memory that stands for a printed word. This auditory memory is supported by muscular, tactile, and even gustatory experiences with the object represented by the word.

Some children have difficulty associating visual symbols with words. Many of these children are aided in recalling the visual symbol for a word by associating its tactile properties (its sensory meaning) with the written symbol. A few are aided by tracing over words while giving the sounds of the word. Others profit from feeling and handling objects— comparing sizes, shapes, texture, and weight—while trying to verbalize the tactile sensations. In this fashion, muscular and tactile sensations, as well as descriptive words, can be associated with common materials, thus strengthening the variety of memories linked to words.

THE CHILD WILL LEARN:

to match shapes by feel
to discriminate textures
to describe orally what he "feels"
to increase vocabulary (spoken and sight) of
    descriptive words

✓ **56.**   Using modeling clay (Plasticene) children roll out long "snakes." They use the long strips to form their names, numerals, other words, or pictures. Immature children may need to follow a model; others may create own words. This activity reinforces the kinesthetic (fine muscle) link to memory.

V **57.**   Attach numerous items of different textures to a large oaktag (or cardboard from a mattress box). Label each item. Encourage children to rub the textures and talk about how they feel. This often leads to interesting language experience stories.

EXAMPLE

"This sheep fur looks like marshmallows, feels like my dog, and smells bad."

V **58.**   Make several "feel-and-guess boxes." Place several items of distinctive shapes and textures in a carton that has a hole cut in the top big enough for a child's hand and lower arm. A child inserts a hand, feeling one item at a time, naming the item, and describing how it feels. After describing the object, the child removes the item to see if he was correct.

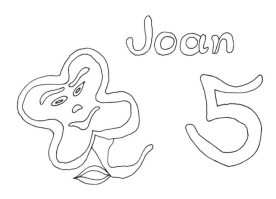

ILLUSTRATION 56.

Four or five children can participate, discussing different reactions to how various items "feel."

√

59.   Fill a large shoebox with items with tactile appeal.
Smaller boxes are labeled with tactile words. Make sure students
can read the labels. Students remove an object from the big box,
examine it, and place it in the appropriate smaller box.

                                                              EXAMPLES

SMOOTH	SOFT	ROUGH
ping pong ball	fur	pot cleaner
small bottle	sponge	fingernail brush
piece of plastic	cotton ball	emery board

60.   To develop awareness of the tactile sense, blind-
fold one child and place an object in his hand, such as a pencil,
pine cone, eraser, or apple. Ask him to identify the object only
by touch.
   Follow-up: When everyone has had a turn, have a
child hold an object in his hand so that the class cannot see it.
As he describes how the object feels, the class can guess what
it is.

61.   Older children may enjoy writing responses to
texture words. Give them several headings as a beginning. They
will add many more. Use examples in the activities above for
starters.

3

Basic Reading Skills

I. LETTER AND WORD RECOGNITION

Rationale

> Word recognition is basic to all levels of reading. Unless the individual can recognize words and their meanings, reading is literally impossible. However, in contrast, letter knowledge is not significant for beginning reading. Word recognition is not aided by being able to name the letters of the alphabet or even the letters within a word. To illustrate, word recognition involves attempting to say a word according to the sounds the letters represent, or their shape, or context of the word, and then, having pronounced it correctly, to recognize it mentally as a meaningful idea (word).

The spelling of the word or naming of the letters does not initiate this recognition-meaning process. Thus, training in the names of letters is preparatory to writing and spelling and preliminary to phonics, but it is irrelevant to the reading act. Only in highly phonic programs must letter names be taught as part of the process of learning to read, and then only to introduce letter sounds.

Some research has attempted to show that knowledge of letter names is highly related to early reading success. The authors of these studies have ignored the fact that such learning is a reflection of the child's cultural background and the education of his parents. Economically deprived children or those not of middle-class background do not know letter names before entering school, for obvious reasons. And no one is so naive as to attribute all the academic difficulties of these children to this oversimplified explanation that letter knowledge means success in beginning reading.

In keeping with current research on methods of beginning reading, letter names may be taught early, but they are taught primarily to permit the rapid introduction of writing, a potent reinforcer of beginning reading. Another argument for teaching letter names early is the marked trend toward introducing more phonics in the beginning stages of reading. These are cogent reasons for teaching letters but not dependent on the argument that they enter into the act of word recognition.

One aspect of the process of word recognition that is often ignored is the difference between meaning words and function words. Nouns and verbs are meaning words with definite mental associations that help the child recognize them. If properly taught with pictorial or action associations, such words are relatively easy to learn. But words like prepositions and conjunctions are almost meaningless, and they are therefore usually difficult to recognize in isolation. Function words are learned by auditory language experiences with phrases and sentences, where they are used in correct, familiar language patterns. When the child is reading, he recognizes to, by, in, or for, not because the word is really meaningful, but because the word would normally occur in the phrase or sentence as he remembers hearing it many times. For these reasons, we do not suggest trying to teach lists of these function words, except in meaningful settings. Once nouns and verbs have been learned through pictures or actions, they can be practiced over again, without these reinforcing clues. But other types of words are not learned by practicing with them in lists. Only by pictures or by use in actual phrases or sentences do function words achieve some degree of meaning and learnability.

THE CHILD WILL LEARN:

to recognize his own name

to recognize labels on common objects

to match and later to name letters in both capital and lowercase forms

to write letters correctly and consistently

to match and compare word shapes

to match and later copy simple words such as nouns and verbs

to recognize simple words in sentences by their shape and/or context

LETTERS AND MATCHING LETTERS

62. Make a large half-moon out of poster paper or colored construction paper. On the moon, print all capital letters of the alphabet. Surrounding the moon, make twenty-six stars, and print one lowercase letter on each. Children match the capital and lowercase letters by attaching yarn from letter to letter. This may be done as a bulletin board or on a smaller scale and enclosed in acetate. If this is done, the children may draw a line with a watercolor marker to connect the letters. To make checking easier, use assorted colors.

63. Make six lotto cards with thirty one-inch squares. Select six letters of the alphabet for each card. Repeat each letter five times on the lotto card. One card and its corresponding

ILLUSTRATION 62.

squares may be a single color, using a different color for the next card and its squares. This keeps each set together.

Show or call out a letter and have the player place a matching letter square on his card. The first player to completely cover his card with squares wins.

VARIATION

> *Use lowercase letters on the cards and capital letters on the individual squares. This game fits nicely in a hosiery or handkerchief box for shelving.*

√ **64.** Join the "carwash!" Draw an automobile on the board and print letters of the alphabet all over it. Each child

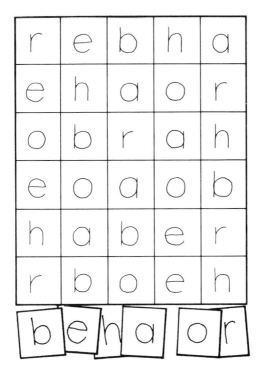

ILLUSTRATION 63.

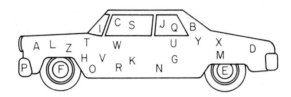

ILLUSTRATION 64.

finds a given letter, says it, then erases it. The object is to wash the car clean. This game may be used for beginning instruction in alphabet recognition or for work in alphabetical order.

WORD RECOGNITION

65. List ten words the children are finding difficult. If a child can correctly read all ten words, he gets to go to the "peppermint tree" for a peppermint or other hard candy. The candy has been tacked to a picture of a tree on the bulletin board.

Yum! Yum!

ILLUSTRATION 65.

66. *Hint:* We realize that consonants give configuration (shape and contour) to words. Thus, consonants are the visual framework of many words. We can often visualize an entire word at a glance, even with all the vowels missing.

67. Write several sentences, as in the examples below. Children try to read them, then write a note to a friend in this fashion.

__t __s r__ __n__ng h__rd. D__d y__ __ br__ng y__ __r __mbr__ll__? __ f__rg__t m__n__, s__ __'ll __s__d n__wsp__p__r __v__r m__ h__ __d.

68. Each child is given a turn as phrase cards are flashed around the group. If he reads the phrase correctly, he remains standing, but if he misses a card, he must stoop. If the child correctly reads the next phrase card before the next child can respond, he rises, and that child stoops. There is no winner in this game. Keep going around the group, but stop before children tire of it.

69. Organize a "label hunt" for primary students. Write a list of commonly used classroom items on the board or on a card at a station. Students locate the labels on the items and match them with the words on the list.

EXAMPLES

rubber cement	chalk
Elmer's glue	poster paint
Crayola	boys (or girls)

70. Reproduce Illustration 70. Place it in a learning station (or on a bulletin board) with a card which says: "Can you put a space ship on the moon by making sentences using all the words on the capsules?" Responses may be written or oral.

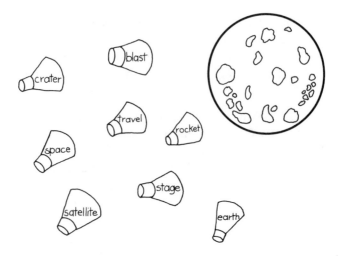

ILLUSTRATION 70.

Children can supply additional interesting words in other categories.

II. CONCEPTS OF READING

Rationale

> There are a number of concepts of using and interpreting books and pictures which are fundamental to the reading act. The most basic of these concepts is the realization that printed words are talking written down. Other basic concepts are the directional flow of ideas in books and pictures, the sequential nature of stories and picture sequences, and the permanance of the word arrangements in a poem or story. Children should also learn to react to stories and pictures, to share their reactions in different ways with other chil-

*dren, and to realize that books and pictures may sug-
gest ideas and actions to the readers.*

*Physical handling of books and pictures,
finding a story by its page number or other means, and
relating the pictures accompanying a story to the ideas
offered in the text are other important concepts of
reading. These ideas must be understood by children
if they are to use books and pictures intelligently and
with pleasure.*

THE CHILD WILL LEARN:

that the words he says can be written down
(and later read)
to recognize the flow of ideas in a book—from
top to bottom, from the beginning to the end,
from left to right
that we can enjoy stories
that we can share our recall of a story or picture
sequence
that pictures accompanying a story tell us
something about the action
that we can do creative things to show our
understanding and enjoyment of reading

DIRECTIONAL ORIENTATION TO
READING

71. Cut out and mount pictures to go with a story,
or draw simple illustrations. After reading the story aloud to the
group, pass out the pictures. Read the story again. While you are
reading, a child stands, holding up his picture, as his scene is
read.

VARIATION

> *Children retell the story, part by part, as they stand with their picture.*

72. Using old magazines, children find pictures of animals, people, cars, or other objects facing left or right and paste them on charts labeled with the directional words.

73. On a piece of oilcloth or solid-color plastic, draw a series of bubbles in a circle. Have these coming from a bubble pipe. In each bubble print a different word or phoneme. Small circles of numbered paper are kept in an envelope. These numbers will tell how many spaces the child is to move. He draws a card and moves his marker the number of spaces indicated. In order to stay on that space, he reads the word printed on the bubble, or, if it is a phoneme, he gives a word containing that phoneme. If he is wrong, he moves back until he lands on a space containing a word he can read. Players take turns, and the game continues until a player reaches the finish line. Additional circles can be made using different words. These may be clipped on for variation.

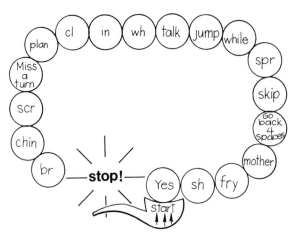

ILLUSTRATION 73.

TELLING, INTERPRETING, AND
RELATING STORIES AND PICTURES

√ **74.**   Choose a story that dramatically narrates varying moods and emotions. Have students skim an assigned passage and identify which of the five senses (smell, taste, touch, hear, see) are evoked and describe how the passage makes them feel. After every portion of the story has been examined, let the class capture the images and emotional tones through an oral reading of the story.

75.   Play a short cartoon film or filmstrip without the sound. The children tell the story from observing the picture sequence.

√ **76.**   When the school or public library is discarding old or damaged children's books, gather as many as you can. Cut out the illustrations and mount them on stiff oaktag. Laminate each sheet, or cover it with clear contact paper. Join the pages as a book. Students use marking pens or crayons to write their versions of a story around the illustrations. It is surprising how many different stories will evolve from one set of illustrations.

III. COMPOSING STORIES AND EXPERIENCE CHARTS

Rationale

> The most realistic approach to beginning reading is through the medium of experience charts. These are group or individual compositions on any subject of interest, written down first by the teacher and later, as they learn to write, by the children themselves. Unlike most reading books, charts provide interesting, varied reading materials that resemble language forms

*and structures already familiar to the children. The
direct connection between reading and speaking is
made obvious, for the children see the very words
they have spoken written on paper. The chart approach makes realistic use of the pupils' auditory
memories for speech and promotes the development
of acquiring thoughts from printed words. A feeling
for sentence structure and sequence is fostered, as is
the habit of reading from left to right. In contrast to
the usual reader, the chart uses real language—
familiar, concrete, and spontaneous.*

*The chart approach equates reading
progress with the child's verbal and thinking skills in
a practical manner. Certainly no child can learn to
read faster than his own experiences and his auditory
and speaking vocabularies permit. This limitation is
recognized most clearly in the experience chart usage,
in contrast to all other methods of beginning reading.
The reading materials that the child gradually learns to
use are created out of his own language ability and
background. Every child learns to read the words he
knows best from his own life experiences. His reading
ability grows with the development of his language
and thinking skills and with his daily experiences—the
only way true reading growth can occur.*

THE CHILD WILL LEARN:

to participate in a group story composition
to recognize the importance of sequence in a
    series of ideas or events
to express his ideas in an organized manner
to recognize various ways of expressing an idea
to visualize ideas in printed form, to connect
    meaning with printed symbols
to understand the concept of a sentence as a
    complete thought

to express his own experiences in writing

to read his own compositions and those of his
    classmates

to use and understand simple punctuation
    (comma, period, question mark, exclamation
    mark)

to read aloud with the usual inflections
    characteristic of speech

COMPOSING STORIES—CREATIVE
WRITING

77. *Hint:* A child's first experience in dictating
stories may be a simple statement, such as "That's me and my
dog playing," when he is drawing a picture. The teacher merely
writes his comment. Or the child relates something that has
occurred, such as "Me and my Daddy went fishing yesterday."
Write his comment without changing his grammar, and suggest
he make a picture to go with his experience.

78. A small group of children chooses a drawing or
picture to discuss. Let them react to the picture in terms of what
is happening. Use their responses to make up a group experience story. Use the children's names, when possible, to enhance
each child's self-concept by seeing his name "in print."

79. Write an experience or class-created story on a
chart or on the board. After it has been read aloud several times,
go through it and erase several words. Have several children
read the story and "think out loud" the missing words as they
go. If you wish to stress one kind of word, such as nouns or
verbs, erase only those words. This activity reinforces visual
memory and use of context clues.

80. Children create their own poems and compile a
class poetry book. Spirit masters may be used. The children can

ILLUSTRATION 80.

type (on a primary typewriter) their own poems or can use their own handwriting.*

√ **81.**   As an independent activity, students may write creative stories or make a picture scrapbook about themselves. A "Just Me" book may include information, such as:*

My family	What I want to be
My favorite things	My funniest dream
My best friend	My feelings about myself

* Submitted by teachers of the James Bowie School, Corsicana, Texas. By permission.

82. Second- and third-graders enjoy making a book-let of "If I could be . . ." stories. Allow each child a half-page spirit master for the completed story. The stories can be dupli-cated so that each child can have a copy of the class project.

Children can make their own bookcovers from con-struction paper.

√ **83.** After a child has written or dictated an experi-ence story, place particular sound elements that are being studied on the board. Children go through their own stories and write down words that contain this element.

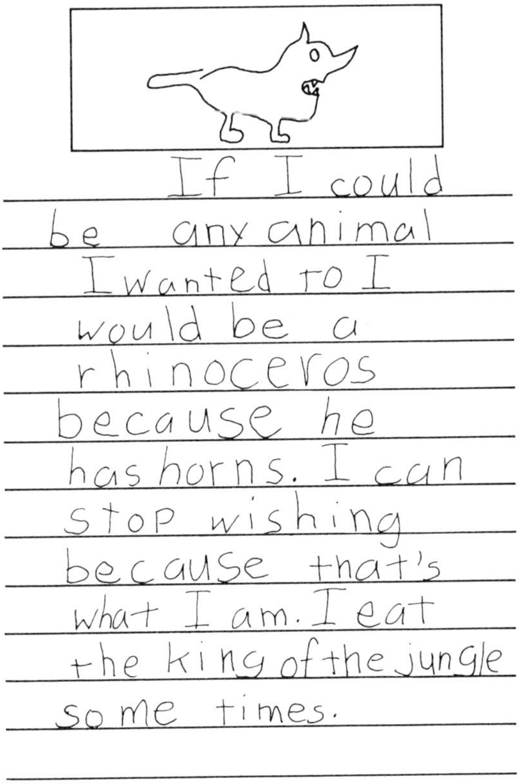

If I could
be any animal
I wanted to I
would be a
rhinoceros
because he
has horns. I can
stop wishing
because that's
what I am. I eat
the king of the jungle
some times.

ILLUSTRATION 82.

VARIATION

> *Circle each plural in green, ing in red, ed in blue.*

84.   *Hint:*   Attach a clothes hanger to an experience chart. This allows the chart to be hung on a chart rack or on a rod as clothes would be hung (see Illustration 84). Dozens of charts can hang this way for easy access.

85.   Make a booklet containing several stories on a particular topic. Topics may be personal experiences, trips, animals, or anything that interests the student.

√ **86.**   A unique way to display creative writing is to use a large picture frame, without the glass. Fold in half a piece of paper the size of the frame. On one half the children write or dictate a story; a crayon drawing or painted illustration is made

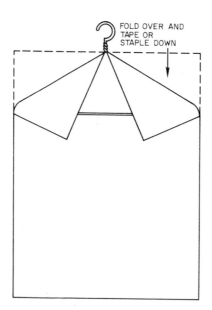

ILLUSTRATION 84.

on the other half. Colored construction paper may be used for background mounting. Display a different story every few days, giving each child an opportunity to share his story. Intermediate level students enjoy this manner of displaying creative writing.

87. Original stories can be presented to small groups by means of puppets, chalk talks, movies, or flannel board. If flannel board is used, construction paper cutouts may be made and adapted for flannel board by gluing small pieces of sandpaper on the backs. Children should also be encouraged to read fiction or fact books and give book reports with these aids.

88. List words on the board that might stimulate a story. Have the words read, then ask a student for a story idea the words suggest. Call on several students for ideas. Each child writes a story, using as many of the words listed on the board as possible. Allow ample time for students to use their creative ideas around the theme (perhaps a day or two).

89. Write several phrases, such as the ones below, on the chalkboard. Children then write a sentence or two on concepts these phrases bring to mind from their own experience. More mature students will expand their ideas into short stories.

EXAMPLES

a falling star	a camel caravan
two birds fighting	a flat tire
Gypsies	catching a fish

90. To stimulate creative writing, make a large "pencil" from a towel roll. Insert a cone shaped from black construction paper for the point. A rubber chair tip can serve as the eraser. Students make up story titles and place these inside the

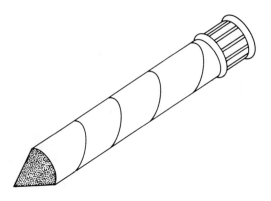

ILLUSTRATION 90.

pencil. As an independent activity, the student may select a title and write a creative story.

91.   Write a short story; the first word beginning with *a*, the second with *b*, and so forth throughout the entire alphabet. The sentences in the story must make sense, and letter order must be maintained.

EXAMPLE

A boy came down every Friday, etc.

92.   Using familiar melodies, students make up creative poems to fit the rhythms of songs.

93.   *Hint:*   Use pictures from old greeting cards as stimuli for creative writing.

94. Records of personal experiences or group projects may be kept in diary form. Organizing material and ideas into this form makes it easy to add information from day to day. After a diary is kept for some kind of class project, the teacher can encourage students to keep reports of personal experiences in diaries of their own. These may be kept at school or at home. If the diaries are to be shared, this activity may be done as a small group activity. Young children can keep picture diaries. A measuring tape and scales may be kept in the room so that children can keep a monthly growth record to include in their diaries.

4

Word
Perception

I. PHONICS

Rationale

> For children who possess the necessary auditory dis-
> crimination ability and vocabulary, phonics can be of
> real assistance in the beginning stages of reading. If
> the child can hear differences between letter sounds
> and learn the common sounds letters represent, he
> may employ these sounds in word recognition. Having
> learned this, he may blend the letter sounds into a
> facsimile of the word. If the word sound is then
> familiar, he may recognize it and comprehend its
> significance in its setting. All this is really the process
> of phonic analysis.

Unfortunately, many teachers of phonics fail to appreciate the interdependence of these behaviors and skills which compose the apparently simple act of recognizing a word through phonic analysis. Many teachers stress only the learning of these sounds as though this were sufficient. They seem unconcerned about whether the child can really discriminate these sounds in reading, writing, speech, and spelling, as well as in phonic exercises. They feel it unimportant that some children do not readily think through words with the aid of auditory images or that children of bilingual or limited background may not have any store of auditory memories for the words in the reader. Some teachers of phonics, as well as some authors of phonics systems, do not appear to realize that skill in blending sounds into recognizable wholes is an essential part of children's training. Finally, even many reading specialists ignore the fact that unless the blended word is quite familiar to the child, phonic analysis fails to produce word recognition. In common primary basal materials, the vocabulary is usually familiar, but in more difficult materials, as in content fields, unfamiliarity of the word or concept may render phonic analysis useless.

Because of these limitations in the usefulness of phonics, we recommend that it be taught only to pupils reading at primary levels. We assume that it is offered solely to those who have (or have learned) adequate auditory discrimination, auditory vocabulary, and an aptitude for using auditory cues to words.

Having taught readers the basic knowledge of letter sounds and blending, two problems remain in applying phonics to the act of reading: the usefulness of phonic principles and the task of making habitual a pattern of phonic attack. Recent research on phonic principles has revealed their applicability in common words taught in the first six grades. We have used this research to select a list of the most *functional rules—those that apply to a reasonably large number of words and that are true more than two-thirds of the time. To ensure the transfer of phonic learning to the reading act, one section is devoted to ways of teaching children a group of practical steps in using phonics to achieve word recognition.*

Since phonics is a rudimentary word perception technique, it must eventually be replaced by more advanced skills, such as syllabication. The introduction of common syllables in the phonic syllabus is, then, a necessary step in this progression. As with phonic rules, these common syllables are carefully selected in terms of their stability and usefulness.

THE CHILD WILL LEARN:

to distinguish the common sounds of single
    letters as they function in words, not merely as
    isolated sounds
to distinguish the sounds of consonant and vowel
    combinations
to recognize that some letters are silent in words
to blend letter sounds and combinations into
    word wholes
to recognize a number of common syllables
to recognize the function of compound words
to apply certain phonic principles
to develop a systematic approach to phonic
    analysis

Phonic Syllabus

Our review of the Clymer, Emans, and Bailey studies
(see Spache and Spache, *Reading in the Elementary School*, third
edition [Allyn and Bacon, Inc.], pp. 463–66) of the utility of
phonic generalizations resulted in an abbreviated phonic
syllabus, using those aids that seem dependable in pronouncing
words.

AT THE PREPRIMER LEVEL:

1. *When the letter c is followed by o or a, the
   sound of k is likely to be heard.*

2. *When there is one e in a word that ends
   in a consonant, the e usually has a short
   sound.*

AT THE PRIMER LEVEL:

3. *When y is the final letter in a word, it has
   a vowel sound.*

4. *When o and a are next to each other in a
   word (e.g.,* boat), *the o is long and the a is
   silent.*

AT THE FIRST READER LEVEL:

5. *When c is followed by e or i, the sound of
   s is likely to be heard.*

6. *When c and h are next to each other, they
   make only one sound.*

7. *Ch is usually pronounced as it is in* kitchen,
   catch *and* church, *not like* sh.
   *(Pronunciations of ch as sh are sometimes
   borrowed from French, as in* Chevrolet.)

8. *When two of the same consonants or
   vowels are side by side, only one is heard.*

9.   *Words having double e usually use the
      long e sound.*

10. *The r gives the preceding vowel a sound
      that is neither long nor short.*

We suggest that as early as possible (for some second-graders), the teacher make a cumulative wall chart, over a period of one or two months, in which one or two of the ten steps below are emphasized each week. After introducing the chart in this manner, it should remain in a highly visible spot on the wall for pupils to use throughout the year. This guide can be of great assistance when students are reading independently. The chart should be in bold print, with key words written in contrasting bright colors for emphasis.

The steps should be discussed and reinforced continually with students so that they fully understand how the chart can aid them.

When You Meet a New Word

1.   *What is the sound of the first letter or
      blend?*

2.   *Finish reading the sentence. What makes
      sense here with this beginning sound or
      blend?*

3.   *How many vowels are there? Where are
      they?*

4.   *If there is one vowel in the beginning or
      middle, try the short sound of the vowel.*

5.   *If there is one vowel and e at the end, try
      the long sound.*

6.   *If there is one vowel at the end, try the long
      sound.*

7.   *If there are two vowels in the middle or
      at the end, try the long sound for the
      first vowel, except in oi, oy, ou, ew, or ui.*

8. *Say the whole word. If this doesn't sound right, try the other vowel sound.*

9. *Now do you know the word? If not, write it down and get help later.*

10. *Go on with your reading!*

INITIAL SOUNDS

95. The old "I spy" game that has been played for generations still has appeal for today's children. Each child in a small group has a turn spying an object which begins with a particular sound. He says "I spy something that begins like *cheese.*" The player who names the correct object then has a turn as leader. Suggest use of an initial or final sound the class has been studying.

96. Complete the words below by supplying the first letter or letters. A student can compare his list with a friend's list to see how they differ and to ascertain if the words are valid. They should come up with as many new words as possible.

_____ump   _____ay   _____at   _____ight   _____ing

97. Another "standing in line" activity. Each child looks around and names something he sees that begins with the same sound as his name. If nothing suitable is in view, he may think of an appropriate word.

98. Using any mail order catalog, students locate pictures of items beginning with certain sounds or blends. A game may be played with two players. Players alternate turns with letters of the alphabet, trying to match pictures with beginning sounds.

99. Make a playing board similar to Illustration 99. Players "snake" their way to the finish line. Use any spinner with up to six numerals. When a player lands on a space, he gives a word beginning with that letter. A few spaces are red, a few green. If he lands on red he must go back two spaces. On green, he gets an extra spin. If the player cannot supply a word, he returns to the last space he was on.

VARIATION

> *To make the game more challenging, the players may give words within a classification, such as:*
>
> clothing   toys
>
> food   people's names
>
> flowers   animals

100. Bingo-style games are old hat, but each new crop of children enjoys these games as much as children did years ago. This Bingo game involves auditory memory, as well as knowledge of initial sounds.

Most games of this type probably would use only consonants. But for students that are doing fairly well in learning phonics, try mixing them. Make as many Bingo-style cards as you

ILLUSTRATION 99.

have children in the small group (as in Illustration 100). Of course, each card will not be identical in the position of the letters. Then from magazines, catalogs, or old workbooks cut clear, simple pictures that begin with the sounds indicated on the cards. Mount these on suitable small cards. As you hold up one picture card at a time, students place a marker on the matching square. The usual Bingo rules apply.

101. Another "waiting in line" activity: The children pretend they are planning a meal. Each child names something to eat beginning with the letter a. When a child cannot think of a food, he must go on to name one starting with b, and the other players follow his lead. If they only get halfway through the alphabet, begin at that point the next time they are waiting in line.

102. Take advantage of your knowledge of children's special interests. Students choose a topic and think of words in

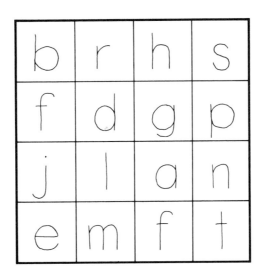

ILLUSTRATION 100.

that area that begin with each sound you are stressing in class. Their responses may grow to be quite a list.

EXAMPLE (cooking)

b	*c*	*fl*
bake	Crisco	flour
butter	cantaloupe	flapjacks
baste	cans	

Other examples: football, fishing, art, clothes, cars, Thanksgiving, Christmas.

103. *Qu* often causes difficulties. After initial instruction in words containing *qu,* write several sentences on the board (or make a spirit master) that require the use of *qu* words.

EXAMPLES

Two pints make one _____ *(quart).*
Opposite of start _____ *(quit).*
A king's wife is called a _____ *(queen).*
Do not be noisy, please be _____ *(quiet).*
A twenty-five cent piece is a _____ *(quarter).*
To be first, you must be _____ *(quick).*

104. Each child writes a short story using as many words containing *qu* as he can. Students share the stories orally, and they often make tongue-twisters.

EXAMPLE

The queen had a quick temper. She often squashed the toes of visiting squires.

BLENDS AND CONSONANT DIGRAPHS

105. Make booklets to show pictures of objects containing consonant digraphs. Make a separate booklet for each digraph. Students cut pictures from magazines and catalogs to paste on the pages. Then the pages may be put together to form booklets. Each picture should be labeled.

Encourage students to use digraphs in various positions, such as *ch*—church, chair, kitchen, punch.

106. Make a mat from a square of oilcloth about fifty-nine inches wide. Divide it into sixteen blocks. In each block, print one of four blends and digraphs with a permanent magic marker. See Illustration 106(a).

Divide a square of tagboard or oilcloth into four sections labeled "left foot," "right hand," "left hand," and "right foot." The four blends are printed in each section, as in Illustration 106(b). Place a commercial spinner in the center.

Make a separate word card for each blend. On each word card, list several words containing that blend, for example, Illustration 106(c).

ILLUSTRATION 105.

One child spins to find the section and blend on which the spinner lands. He then selects a word from the appropriate word card and says it. Two other children find the blend and place the appropriate hand or foot in the proper square. The game continues until one child loses his balance and falls or gives an incorrect response. Only three children may play at a time. This game is best done barefoot.

107. Cut a circle out of cardboard. Using a felt-tip marker, write consonant blends around the circle. The children sit around the circle and take turns flipping a small stone, a chip, or a coin in the air, letting it land on the cardboard. The child has to think of a word that has the blend on which the pebble fell.

Mat

br	ch	dr	st
st	br	ch	dr
dr	st	br	ch
ch	dr	st	br

ILLUSTRATION 106 (A).

108. Cover a large cardboard disc from a pizza package with cloth, paper, or plastic. (Or, if new, it can remain un-

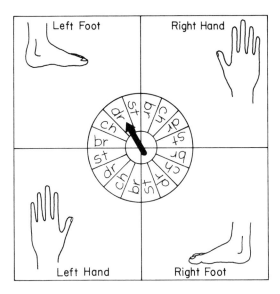

ILLUSTRATION 106 (B).

dress drink

drop drive

ILLUSTRATION 106 (C).

covered.) Around the outside edges, print some blends or digraphs. Place a spinner in the center. Let a small group of children take turns spinning the hand and giving a word beginning or ending with the sound indicated.

EXAMPLE

wh	*fl*	*cr*	*gr*
white	fly	crow	green
whistle	flop	cry	grow
why	flutter	cross	grass

109. Students choose a topic they are interested in and list words in this topic that contain consonant digraphs.

EXAMPLE (food)

ch	*sh*
spinach	squash
cheese	shellfish

The Index in a cookbook will be helpful.

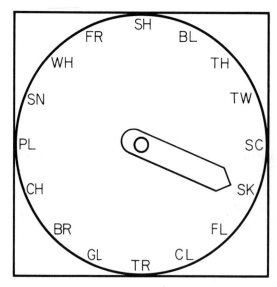

ILLUSTRATION 108.

SHORT AND LONG VOWELS

110. "Red Baron Says" can be played to check students' knowledge of sounds, endings, syllables, or other language skills. Give each player a small card with *yes* written on one side and *no* on the other side. The teacher will make a statement. If the information is true, the players put their *yes* card up; if it is false, they put up their *no* card. If a child gives an incorrect response, he is out until the next game. The last person remaining in the game is the winner.

EXAMPLE

Red Baron says, "Short a says ā."   (*no*)
Red Baron says, "long e as in beat."   (*yes*)

111. From magazines or catalogs cut out simple pictures that clearly indicate the vowel sounds you want to stress. Place these pictures on a chart, bulletin board, or flannel board. In a box nearby, place word cards the children have studied. They go through the cards and tack (or adhere in some way) the words with the same vowel sound under each picture having that sound.

For self-checking, write the vowel sound on the back of each word card.

112. Divide the group into teams of no more than four members each. Each team is given a sheet of words with the vowels missing. Members work together to list as many different words as possible using different vowels. When the time limit is up, the teams exchange papers to check validity. The dictionary may be used for verification of words.

EXAMPLES

—t   t__p (e)   cl__p   m__k__   r__g

113.   Whatever story the child is reading can be used to review phonic skills. Select any page from the story. Each word on the page that contains the specified phonic element is written on a paper. If the story isn't too long, use the entire story.

114.   A sheet of paper or a transparency may be divided into squares. In each square draw an object that illustrates a vowel sound. Ask the child to look at the picture and indicate the vowel sound heard in the word by filling the letter in the blank. If students are advanced enough, they may use the long (–) or short (◡) marks also. The sheet may be covered with acetate or may be laminated for repeated use. Put the answers on the reverse side (or on an overlay) for self-checking.

115.   Substitute numbers for vowels. Children may find it fun to make up their own code to use in the place of vowels.

ILLUSTRATION 114.

---

a	e	i	o	u
2	3	4	5	6

Th3 d5g b2rk3d 2t m3.

116. Have pupils in the group think of animals that contain different sounds of *o* in their names.

---

oo	ō	o
moose	goat	fox
goose	mole	dolphin

VARIATION

> *Any vowel sounds may be used. Other classifications can also be used, such as flowers, vegetables, or clothing.*

117. *Hint:* * The most common vowel sound is the schwa (*uh*). It can be spelled with any of the letters representing vowels. When there is a vowel in an unaccented syllable, it usually is the ə (uh) sound.

Using a page from the child's reader, instruct him to list all words containing the schwa (*uh*) sound.

VARIATION

> *Students list the vowels across the top of their paper. Under each vowel they list words containing that vowel pronounced as the schwa (uh) sound. An entire story will be needed as a source for words.*

---

* Adapted from an activity submitted by Nancy Bowden, University of Houston, Houston, Texas. By permission.

SILENT LETTERS

118. Make a permanent chart showing how the silent e sometimes changes the pronunciation of a one-syllable word. *Caution:* This principle is valid less than half the time, so choose your words carefully, and use it as an aid only, not as a phonic rule.

See Activity 456 for description of window shade charts.

119. Flash cards can be made from oaktag. Punch a hole in the card to the left of the word. On the front of each card write a base word or a word that can be changed by adding the letter e. On the back of the card, write an ending or the letter e so that when the card is folded, the ending (or the e) touches the base word. Let the children practice making new words by adding endings or by changing the word with the addition of the silent e. These cards can be stacked on a note spindle.

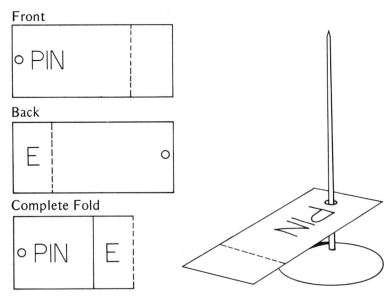

Front

o PIN

Back

E   o

Complete Fold

o PIN   E

ILLUSTRATION 119.

120. Two or four students can play this game. Make a game board, as in Illustration 120, on either cardboard or a sheet of heavy plastic. A player spins the arrow and makes a sentence with the word as it appears on the game board, then makes another sentence with the word after the silent e is added. If the player cannot give a correct sentence, each opponent receives an extra point.

121. Bring several newspapers to class. Children choose an article and circle all the words in it that contain silent letters. They may then exchange articles; the partner marks through all the silent letters in the marked words. Students check their partner's work both ways.

122. On the board, write a list of words containing silent letters. These may be vowels or consonants or both. Make sure you have discussed the rules of silent letters prior to this activity. Students copy the words and mark out the silent letters

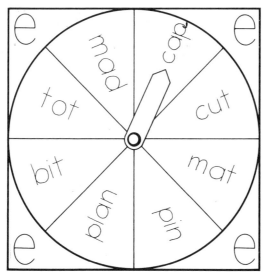

ILLUSTRATION 120.

with a crayon or colored pencil (this makes them easier to check).

VARIATION

> *You can do this with a transparency on the overhead projector and use an overlay with the marks for correction.*

EXAMPLES

cak̸e   me̷at   bal̸l
go̸at   gro̸w   knif̸e

123.   Following a lesson on silent letters, review the fact that the *gh* is silent in words containing *igh* (*high*, for example). It usually is fun to write a short story using as many *igh* words as possible. The next day several students may want to read their stories to the class. While the stories are being read, a student can record each *igh* word on the board. It is surprising how many they will use.

BLENDING SOUNDS INTO WORDS

124.   Draw three circles on the board (see Illustration 124). Put consonants in the first circle, vowels in the second, and consonants in the third. The child makes a word by using a letter from each circle to form the beginning, middle, and final sounds of a word. Then he blends the words and writes them on paper.

EXAMPLES

bay   tar   put   can   meat   pain

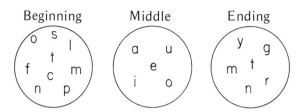

Beginning   Middle   Ending

ILLUSTRATION 124.

125. A sense of fun and an attractive display stimulate interest in learning. Draw a butterfly on the board with syllables on its wings, as in Illustration 125. Children blend these syllables into words and write the words on their papers. They can compare lists to see if they have blended syllables into all possible word combinations. As a variation, some children may want to create a design with syllables for other children to blend. This would provide excellent practice in using the dictionary to determine how to break words into syllables.

126. This activity should probably be classified as spelling, but blending is certainly evident. Collect used flash

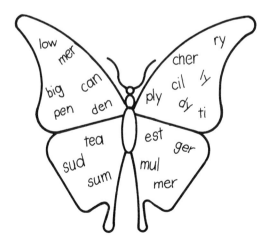

ILLUSTRATION 125.

cubes from students' parents. Cover each cube with paper or tape. On each side of every cube, print a different letter of the alphabet. A permanent felt-tip marker may be used. Vowels and common consonants should be duplicated often. Then cut the top from a plastic bleach bottle to use as a container for the covered cubes. Each child takes a turn and spills the cubes from the container. Without turning any cubes over, he makes as many words as he can with the letters showing. A point is allowed for each word formed. Time may be kept by using a one-minute egg timer.

VARIATION

> *Print words on each cube. Players make sentences using as many cubes as they can.*

127.   Cut small squares from oaktag and print a letter on each. Make several squares for each letter of the alphabet. Blends or digraphs may also be printed on the cards. Sort the cards alphabetically and keep them in separate compartments of

ILLUSTRATION 126.

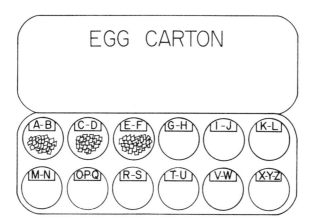

ILLUSTRATION 127.

an egg carton. Let children practice forming words by taking the letters from the carton and laying them out on a desk. Stress making words they know or have heard before, and have them build the words from memory. Word parts (syllables) may be also used instead of letters.

128. Prepare a 5 × 8 card instructing the student to blend as many words as possible with word parts. Students write their words on a pad of paper placed with the card. Some possible words may be written on the back of the card for self-checking. Tape a flap over the list so the student must lift it to see answers.

EXAMPLES

ch	air
bl	ack
gr	own
p	ast
st	it

129.   This activity combines blending word parts into words and the use of context clues. Write several paragraphs with many parts of words missing. Supply the word parts that may be used to blend them into words. The sample paragraph could be extended, using the same list of word parts.

---

*We cooked din_____ on the gr_____. We
had st_____, ap_____, po_____toes,
br_____, but_____, m_____ and ice
cr_____. It was a good _____nic but Dad
sp_____ed some cr_____ on my h_____.
Mom wanted to _____ke a _____ture of me
as it _____eamed down my h_____. But I
scr_____ed "NO!"*

ner	ead	eak	ta	ples	str
ill	pic	ter	ilk	eam	

VOWEL DIGRAPHS AND DIPHTHONGS

130.   Use any kind of illustration and write the desired diphthong or vowel digraph on each. Make lines for students to write words containing the sounds. It is best either to duplicate the papers or to have several laminated for easy wipe-off. In the latter case, place possible answers on the reverse side of the card.

131.   This is an activity to give practice using the two sounds for *oo*. Write a *oo* word for each meaning. Children will add to the list from their independent reading.

ILLUSTRATION 130.

EXAMPLES

Part of a house _____ (room).
Middle of the day _____ (noon).
One who prepares food _____ (cook).
Not warm _____.
Part of a plant _____.
In a short time _____.
Part of black smoke _____.
Sweep with it _____.

132. To make learning more effective, we must relate the spoken word to an object, where possible, and then to the printed word. This activity follows such a procedure. Collect small items that call attention to sound elements you want to emphasize. Spread these items on the table where the group is sitting. Pronounce a sound (such as $\bar{a}i$). A student finds an object containing that sound, names the item, holds it up, then replaces it on the table. Any sound element may be used, but a few examples for vowel digraphs and diphthongs are below. After the word is pronounced, the teacher holds up a card with the word printed on it or writes the word on the board.

EXAMPLES

ai	*(sail, mail, nail)*
ea	*(heads, seat, peach)*
oy-oi	*(boy, toy, oil, foil)*
ōw (ow)	*(bow, cow, towel)*

VARIATION

> *Word cards may be distributed to students in advance, and when a student's word is named, he holds up the card.*

133. *Hint:* The sound of *r* is not present as a single sound when it occurs in the middle or at the end of the word because it follows a vowel and is modified by it. Therefore, the vowel preceding *r* is neither long nor short, but *r*-controlled.

as in floor: score, tore, more, four.
as in poor: sure, cure, moor.
as in hear: fear, steer, clear, peer.
as in heard: bird, shirt, word, hurt, herd.
as in there: share, bare, fair, pair.
as in start: cart, guard, garden, heart.

FINAL SOUNDS

134. Make a rectangle of stiff cardboard. Draw lines that divide the top and bottom of the card into equal sections (see Illustration 134). Words or pictures are placed on the top row, and the answers are placed in a different order on the bottom. Punch holes in each section. Using string or yarn, the child matches a word from the top row with one on the bottom.

VARIATION

> *This activity may be used for math, language arts, science, or social studies or as an aid in visual-motor development.*

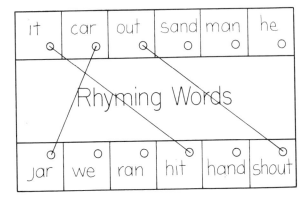

ILLUSTRATION 134.

Also, the board can be changed by making more words on paper and attaching them to the board with paperclips.

135. Using a board like the one in Activity 134, ask children to add more pairs of words that rhyme. They first can do this first orally, then on the chalkboard.

EXAMPLE

pool	school
bean	clean
scratch	hatch
noose	moose

136. To develop awareness of the positions of letter sounds in words, have students draw three columns on their papers. Label the columns "beginning," "middle," and "end." As the teacher says a word, the student draws a line to the column that represents where in the word is the letter sound designated by the teacher. Or the student can write the symbols in the correct column. Be sure students understand which sound they are listening for.

EXAMPLE

	Beginning	*Middle*	*End*
stand			
fast			
poster			
faster			
stem			

137. Divide the class into two teams, which line up facing each other. The first player on one team pronounces a word, such as *want,* and uses it in a sentence.The first player on the opposing team then says a word that begins with the ending sound of the previous word, such as *team,* and uses it in a sentence. The next player says a word beginning with an *m* sound, and so on. A child who fails to make a correct response adds a point to his team's score. The team with fewer points is the winner. Caution children to use words which begin like the other word sounds, not like it is spelled. If one child uses the word *cake,* the opposing player should omit the silent *e* and use a word beginning with a *k* sound.

PHONOGRAMS

138. An overhead transparency can be made to review sounds. Rule the transparency into six or eight squares. Draw illustrations in each square of objects that use the sounds being reviewed. Under the picture in each square, write the name of the object, omitting the letters of sounds being stressed. Have a child come to the overhead projector and complete the word by filling in the missing letter or letters. You can omit initial consonants, blends, digraphs, or you can give the initial sound and omit phonograms.

139. List several words on the board. Give students a piece of paper and have them write as many rhyming words as they can for each word on the board. Encourage them to write as many as they can without help, then draw a line after the last one written in each column and list after that the rhyming words they have found in reading material, for instance, spelling books. Words need not conform to spelling patterns.

can—*fan, ran, man, pan, ban, Nan, tan, van, plan*
   (*swan not acceptable*).
dog—
clay—*day, prey, sleigh.*
and—

140.   Instructional aid.   The bookworm (Illustration 140) is excellent for displaying rhymes. Each hump bears a word that rhymes with words printed on other humps. The bookworm is mainly for display areas such as bulletin boards. Use any phonogram you are currently studying. See how long the worm can grow.

141.   Use your science or social science text to reinforce rhyming. Write a number of words on the board that have many possibilities for rhyming. Students use one of the lessons in their textbooks to locate rhyming words. Students should record the page number containing the word to be rhymed.

high	*page #*	*clay*	*page*
my	_____	*gray*	_____
fry	_____	*sleigh*	_____

ILLUSTRATION 140.

142. On any size cards you have an abundance of, print words such as these, one word to a card:

bill	fat	hall	free	fight
still	sat	ball	see	sight
fill	bat	fall	he	height
bill	hat	stall	bee	bite

Print several cards with the word *free.* Shuffle all the cards together. Deal five cards to each player, and place the rest of the deck on the table, face down. Instruct the first child to lay down a card and name the word; the next player lays down a card that rhymes *or* that begins with the same letter as the first word, for example: If the first player laid down *hill,* the second might play *still* or *hat.*

When a player cannot play from the cards in his hand, he draws from the deck until he can play or until he has drawn three cards. If he has a "free" card he may use that card for any word in his hand. The first player to get rid of all his cards wins the game. If the dual rules are too complicated for the children, simply use either rhyming or beginning sounds.

143. Give students sentence clues that describe words. Tell students which phoneme they are to use in their answer. The teacher may read the sentences aloud or duplicate them for a written activity. Some students may want to write clues for others to complete.

In each answer to the following clues, you hear the word *at.* This is a fun way to review rhyming words and phonograms.

EXAMPLE

A disagreement is called a ___at.
A domestic animal that chases mice is a ___at.
You wear it on your head. ___at.
Answers: spat, cat, hat.

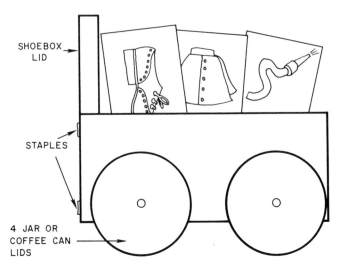

SHOEBOX
LID

STAPLES

4 JAR OR
COFFEE CAN
LIDS

ILLUSTRATION 144.

144. Use a mail-order catalog to cut out pictures of items that might be found in a particular department of a store, for example, clothing, toys, hardware. Paste the pictures on cards and distribute them randomly to the group. The teacher calls out a retail department and a word, as: *hardware—rose.* A player holds up a rhyming word in that department, as: *hose.* This player places his picture card in a box labeled "shopping cart." The player wins who runs out of picture cards first.

II. STRUCTURAL ANALYSIS

Rationale

Another fundamental approach to word recognition is through structural analysis. This involves reacting to words in terms of their inflectional endings, internal changes in sound and spelling, and simple prefixes and suffixes. Such analysis also demands the recognition that two words may be telescoped into one, as in contractions, or added together to form a compound word. It does not include the attempt to recognize small words within larger ones. This technique fails because of the variations in pronunciation of common words appearing to function as syllables. The influence of accent, or the loudness of syllables within a word, is a minor facet of structural analysis. Finally, there are a few principles of structural analysis for which the research indicates some practical usefulness.

THE CHILD WILL LEARN:

to recognize the effect of inflectional endings
upon word meaning
to recognize the effect of simple prefixes upon
word meaning
to be familiar with internal changes in words in
spelling and pronunciation
to use accent as an aid to correct pronunciation
to recognize common contractions
to apply certain structural principles
to recognize compound words

CONTRACTIONS

145. After working with the contracted form of *not,* the following exercise may be used. Help children give contractions in which not is shortened. The following list may appear on the board:

will not	would not	were not
is not	had not	has not
should not	have not	does not
can not	was not	
did not	could not	

146.   Write a one-paragraph story calling for many contractions. Students fill in the blanks with the missing contractions. Capable students may enjoy making up similar stories.

EXAMPLE

I _____ feeling very well. My throat hurts,
so I _____ talk very loudly. I _____ take
my medicine, so Mom said she _____ let me
talk on the phone. I sure _____ do that
again. Maybe _____ be better tomorrow.

147.   Tape record the voices of a group of students in conversation. Any situation will do: committee work, playing a game, and so on. Do not let students know that the purpose of the taping is to record contractions they may use. Later, play the tape and ask that they *listen* for contractions. As each contraction is noticed, write it on the board. Follow this with a discussion of what words were combined to make each contraction.

148.   Many basal readers avoid contractions up to the third-year level. (I don't understand why, as contractions are commonly used.) Ask students to search through the library book they are reading and note all the contractions they encounter. They might also copy the sentences where contractions are used. These lists may then be discussed in a small group. Give attention to colloquial expressions that may appear, such as the examples of acceptable dialect, below.

ain't	tain't	ya'll
hain't	been't	d'ruther
cain't	I'se	t'uther

COMPOUND WORDS

149. *Hint:* True compound words are not merely two separate words put together to form a new word. A compound word consists of two words that are joined to describe an object or expression in which each word retains its original meaning. Many commercial phonic programs will probably disagree with this, as they seem to tag every word made up of two small words as compounds.

Valid: steamboat, housefly, railroad.
Invalid: forget, into, before, understood, below.

150. Students look for compound words they can illustrate humorously. After many have been compiled, make a large chart or a booklet to show their work.

151. This activity draws attention to how compound words are formed. On 3 × 5 cards print compound words, then cut between the two words that form the compound. Place the sections in an envelope and have students fit the two parts of a compound together, making as many correct words as they can. Then direct students to write these words on a sheet of paper.

doorbell

fishnet

cowboy

ILLUSTRATION 150.

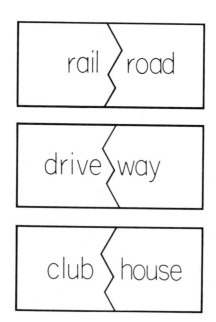

ILLUSTRATION 151.

152. Prepare a rather long list of words made of two or more words. Some of these will be true compounds (see Hint 149, above) and others will not be true compounds. Students indicate the true compounds.

EXAMPLES

clubhouse	forgot	bookworm
wallpaper	houseboat	below
watchband	afterward	racetrack
behind	without	fishnet
until	together	anything
another	treehouse	gentleman

153. Write words that could be part of compound words on one hundred or more small blank cards. Each of four players is dealt eight cards. The remainder are placed in a stack in the center. The first player places one card from his hand face up. The player on his left uses a card from his hand to make a compound. If he cannot, he draws a card from the stack and the next player continues. The first player to use all his cards wins.

VARIATION

> *May be played using opposites, synonyms, and other ways to match words.*

ACCENT

154. *Hint:* Words that are spelled alike but that have different meanings, and sometimes have different pronunciations, are called *homographs*. It is fun to work with homographs because you can make such interesting sentences. Only the context gives a clue to the word's pronunciation, unless an accent mark is evident.

155. List sentences on the board or on a ditto sheet. Use a pair of homographs (words with the same spelling, different meanings, and sometimes different pronunciations) in each. By studying the context, students can determine the pronunciation and place the accent mark in the correct place. The dictionary may be used to check pronunciations.

---

1. Father was present to presént the gifts.
2. The farmers were not able to prodúce enough próduce for the market.
3. The author was contént with the cóntent of his article.
4. If you do not addréss the letter correctly, it may not be delivered to the right áddress.
5. The manager will objéct to this óbject being in the office.

156. Upper-grade students benefit from making their own sentences using homographs. The sentences should clearly indicate which pronunciation is correct. The dictionary will be in constant use during this activity. You may want to request that the students mark the accents in the two-syllable words.

---

wind	live	excuse	convict
conduct	annex	subject	close
refuse	rebel	contract	address
lead	read	produce	permit
perfect	object	combine	content

157. Upper-grade students may have fun writing a silly paragraph using many words that have more than one pronunciation. The student then reads his paragraph orally to the group, using the wrong pronunciation for each homograph. This should bring many chuckles from the group.

ROOTS, PREFIXES, SUFFIXES, AND
INFLECTIONAL ENDINGS

158. Instructional aid. A chart or ditto may be made, asking for comparison in size or degree. After each question, draw three varied objects. Use such questions as, "Which is the smallest?" "Which is the brightest?" or "Which is the largest?" This activity is best used in a small discussion group.

VARIATION

> *The worksheet may be placed in an acetate folder
> so that students can mark on it and wipe it off.*

159. Explain that when there are *two* objects, one can be *taller* than the other. But when there are *three or more* objects one can be *tallest*. Write several comparative adjectives on the board. Students choose four of them to illustrate on drawing paper.

EXAMPLES

tall	low	fat
short	cold	funny
high	wet	long

160. Children make new words by adding *er* and *est* to each root word that the teacher writes on the board. They use each new word in a sentence. Additional practice should be given by using these words in their written work. Words extracted from the science lesson serve a dual purpose.

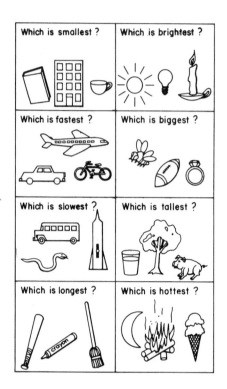

ILLUSTRATION 158.

EXAMPLE

new   _____   _____
quiet   _____   _____
cool   _____   _____

161.   Words that are composed of a root plus a suffix may be listed on the board or shown on an overhead projector. Students write or say aloud two sentences for each word: one sentence with the root word and one with the root plus the suffix.

walking   greatest
quickly   teacher
calls   balanced

162. Some prefixes added to a word cause it to mean the opposite of the base word. Give the children a list of such root words. Words requiring different prefixes to change the meaning may be listed together. Prefixes such as *dis, ir,* or *il* may be needed. The children then give a sentence orally or in writing to show they comprehend the meaning of the word.

Add *un* to these: lock, hitch, kind.

163. Give students a list of sentences on dittoed sheets, and ask them to write in the words that belong in the blanks, using the correct prefix or suffix where needed to complete the sentence. Also caution students to watch for the correct *tense.* Leave space below your list for students to write their own sentences using the prefixes and suffixes stressed in class.

It is _____ to cross the street without looking.
    (safe)
The man was the _____ one in the contest.
    (fast)
I was the _____ one to find a dime. (luck)
We were _____ when our dog died. (happy)

164.   To develop students' ability to guess the meaning of words made from root words they know, write pairs of sentences on the board to be read aloud. Students identify the derivative and discuss how its meaning has been altered in relation to the root word.

He spends much time in study.
He is a studious boy.

She will receive the prize.
She was the recipient of the prize.

It will please me to go to the party.
It was a pleasant party.

165.   A letter or syllable added to the end of a word can change the meaning of the word. The suffixes *er* and *or* mean "one who does something." Give each child a dittoed list of words, similar to those below, whose meanings are changed by the addition of *er* or *or*. The student writes the proper word for each item. This activity may also be done aloud with a small group.

---

one who visits	one who plays
one who teaches	one who seeks
one who leads	one who directs
one who hunts	one who instructs
one who dreams	one who drives

166.   Using a stack of small cards, print on each card a derived word, for example, *untrue, thoughtless, greenish, friendly, action.* On the reverse side of each card, print the root word. Stack the cards in the center of a table, with the derived words face up. Instruct the first player to take a card, read the derived word, and name the root word. If he is correct, he keeps the card; if he fails to name the correct root word, the card is placed at the bottom of the stack. The next player takes a turn, and the game ends when all cards are used. The player with the most cards is the winner.

167. List some root words on the board. Then list some prefixes or suffixes. Students match a root word with a prefix or suffix and use it in a sentence. The same word and ending may not be used twice. Be sure to keep vocabulary within students' experiences.

EXAMPLES

quick	ly
homesick	able
kind	er
weak	est
dead	less
like	ness
comfort	

168. Discuss with the class the changing of a word's meaning by putting a syllable (prefix) in front of the word. Then give each student a list of words whose meanings become opposite when a prefix is added, as in the examples below. Instruct students to change the meanings of the words by adding one of the following prefixes: *un, im, dis, in*. Then students use each new word in a meaningful sentence.

EXAMPLES

accurate	correct	accurate
safe	sure	convenient
possible	continue	certain
grateful	clean	willing

169. This is similar to Activity 168. Give students a list of words and tell them to write the *base word* for each in an interesting sentence, for instance, *elves*—the elf was a funny little guy.

EXAMPLES

cries	forgiving
unhappy	disbelief
funniest	balloons
dresses	teacher

170. Bingo-type games may be used for practice in many areas. They may be used with initial sounds and blends or with prefixes and suffixes. For the prefix–suffix game, write root words across the top of a card, and in the squares below write prefixes, suffixes, or both, as in Illustration 170. When a word is called, the player looks down the column under the root word to find the prefix or suffix needed. He then places a disc in that square. If the word called contains both a prefix and a suffix, the player's space must contain both in order for him to claim the word. Regular Bingo rules are followed.

VARIATION

> For more advanced students, mix the endings and omit the root words from the card.

171. After class discussion, make a chart showing suffixes and prefixes learned. Many words may change meanings when a prefix or suffix is added. List these words on small slips of paper. Instruct each child to draw a specified number of slips. Using suffixes and prefixes, the child makes as many words as possible, bringing his list to be discussed the following day. This is a meaningful outside assignment.

Note: You may want students to use each word in a written sentence to show how the meaning changes.

Prefix - Suffix Bingo

pay	spell	lock	joy	please
re	mis	ing	en	dis
ing	re	un	ful ly	ing
pre	mis ed	re	ful	dis ing
ment	ing	un ed	en ment	ing ly

ILLUSTRATION 170.

EXAMPLE

Place: *replace, unplaced, displaced, placed, places*

172. List several new words from a social studies lesson. Students underline the prefixes and suffixes and write sentences to show the meaning of the words within the context of the topic under discussion.

EXAMPLES

*un*changed   predictable
*de*central*ize*   unlawful

173. This game is competitive and best used with capable fifth- and sixth-graders. Divide the class into two teams, and assign each team a section of the chalkboard. Write a prefix on the board, for example, *mis, dis,* or *re.* Instruct the first member of one team to take his place at the board and write a word that begins with the designated prefix. For example, if the teacher had written *mis,* the child might write *mislead.* An opposing team member then has a turn, and the teams alternate writing words. When one player cannot think of a word, the other team gets an extra turn. When neither team can think of a word, use a new prefix.

174. *Hint:* In order for children to use plurals correctly in creative writing, make a colorful chart with the following information:

Making Plurals

1. *Regular nouns add* s.   (caps)
2. *Nouns ending in* s, ch, sh, *or* x *add* es.
   (dishes, boxes)
3. *Nouns ending in* y *preceded by a vowel add* s.   (days)
4. *Nouns ending in* y *preceded by a consonant change to* ies.   (babies)
5. *Nouns ending in* f *or* fe *usually change to* ves.   (calves)
6. *Some nouns become different words.*
   (mouse—mice; man—men)
7. *Some nouns do not change.*   (sheep, deer)
8. *Some nouns change some of the time.*   (fish—fish *if all of one kind,* fishes *if several kinds together*)

175. Divide the class into two teams. Say slowly—but only once—three nouns, such as *house, toy, girl.* Then, direct the first player on one team to say the plurals of these words in the same sequence. Teams alternate answering until every child has had a turn. A team gets one point for each correct plural given in the right sequence. The team with the most points wins. After the first round is over, begin the second by naming three nouns whose plurals are irregularly formed, such as *mouse, half, leaf.*

176. Write on the board a list of words whose plurals are variously formed. The class says or writes the correct plural for each word and gives the correct spelling.

EXAMPLES

shelf	moose	woman
potato	baby	donkey

177. List several words on the board. Then ask which words can be changed by adding *s*. The ending is added in colored chalk. Continue using as many endings as possible. If one word can take several endings, it is rewritten each time, using the new ending. Be sure to include a few words that are not appropriate for the ending, such as *happy*.

EXAMPLES

play	happy	smile
got	run	and

178. Each student may skim through a story in his library book to locate words in the singular that would have odd plural spellings. Then he makes a list of these words, writes his name on the list, and drops it into a box. Later, each child draws a slip from the box, writes the correct plural of each word on the list, then returns it to the originator for checking.

179. Write several paragraphs on two-thirds of a spirit master. Omit inflectional endings such as tense and plurals. Students fill in the endings on the dittoed sheets. On the lower, blank third of the paper, the student makes up a paragraph in the same manner. The pages are then exchanged by students. Each checks the top of the paper he received and completes the bottom portion. Then he signs it and returns it to the originator.

III. SYLLABICATION

Rationale

The purpose of syllabication is to enable the reader to pronounce the parts of a word and thus, hopefully, to recognize the word. Actually, many rules of syllabication commonly taught are really aids in dividing a word at the end of a line and have little to do with pronunciation. For example, the priniciple that double consonants are usually divided into the two adjoining syllables, as in but-ter, *is simply a writing convention and has nothing to do with pronunciation. Moreover, like phonic rules, principles of syllabication vary greatly in their validity—in the proportion of times they actually apply. Some are always true, but others function in less than half the words in which we might expect them to. We have tried to confine our exercises to the application of the most useful principles of syllabication.*

THE CHILD WILL LEARN:

to recognize and pronounce common syllables
to apply a few basic syllabication principles

to divide words into syllables, pronounce the
separate parts, and blend them into a whole
word

to use syllabication systematically as an aid to
pronunciation

Syllabication Syllabus

We do not believe in the memorization of syllabication principles. The concepts involved should be derived inductively from lessons planned to help pupils observe those concepts. The generalizations derived from these lessons should be kept as few and as simple as possible. Only generalizations that clearly help in pronouncing a word should be emphasized. The purpose of this training is to gain a few basic concepts of how words may be divided into syllables in an attempt to pronounce them—*not* to produce perfect word division. In keeping with this reasoning, we suggest the following principles:

1. *Every syllable has a vowel sound in it.*

2. *When the first vowel sound is followed by* th, ch, *or* sh, *these combinations are not divided and may go with the first or second syllable (for example,* ma-chine, moth-er).

3. *When the first vowel sound in a word is followed by two consonants, the first syllable usually ends with the first of these consonants (for example,* bul-let, pic-ture).

4. *When the first vowel sound is followed by a single consonant, that consonant usually begins the second syllable (for example,* sta-tion, la-dies, ta-ble).

5. *In most two-syllable words, the first syllable is accented (for example,* háp-py, pén-cil).

6. *When a prefix is added to a root word, the root word is usually accented (for example, in-side, dis-co-lor).*

7. *If a, in, re, ex, de, or be is the first syllable in a word, it is usually accented (for example, a-ble, in-ter-est, re-cent, de-cent, bet-ter). However, when these same syllables are prefixes, they are not accented (for example, be-side, re-claim, in-vis-i-ble, pre-scribe).*

Our third syllabication principle implies that the vowel usually has a short sound. The fourth principle implies that the open syllable usually has a long vowel sound.

DIVISION OF SYLLABLES

180. With a small group, the teacher pronounces a word. Each child holds up a small numbered card that tells how many parts are in that word. For example, if the word *cowboy* were called, the child would hold up the card showing the number 2. After children have become familiar with small words, they may enjoy determining the number of syllables in such words as *rhi-no-cer-os* or *u-ku-le-le*.

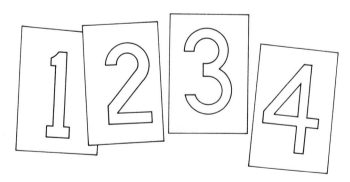

ILLUSTRATION 180.

181. Rule a piece of paper into squares. Draw an object in each square. Pupils sound the word phonetically and write it by syllables under the picture.

182. Children make a large, colorful wall chart listing all of their names by the number of syllables.

EXAMPLE

one	two	three
Joe	Ag-nes	Ev-e-lyn
Stan	San-dy	Ro-ber-ta
George		

pen-cil	bi-cy-cle	book
tel-e-phone	flow-er	glass-es
ta-ble	in-vi-ta-tion	shoe

ILLUSTRATION 181.

183. On any size cards, list a vocabulary word on each card. On the back of the card, write the number of syllables in that word. Keep the set together with a rubber band or in an envelope. This activity is best done with two players. One child holds up a card, with the word facing his partner. The partner reads the word, then tells how many syllables it contains. He then turns the card over to see if his answer is correct.

184. Choose multisyllabic words from the health or science texts the students are using. They should be words the students have discussed during the lesson. List the words down the left side of a sheet of paper. Draw lines to the right of each word for the students to write in the number of syllables. If you make several copies and place them in acetate folders, the answers can be placed on the back for self-checking.

EXAMPLES

vessel _____2_____
vein _____
skin _____
fingernail _____
cuticle _____

185. Students choose a page (or are assigned a page) in their social studies textbook. Each student makes four columns on a sheet of notebook paper. All one-syllable words are recorded in the first column, two syllables in the next, and so on. They should not record any word more than once.

186. Use a common spinner with numerals from 1 to 4. Four of five students take turns turning the spinner. When it stops on a numeral, the student must say a word with that num-ber of syllables.

Vocabulary from a particular category should be used,

as in the example below. Words may not be reused. Score may be kept.

EXAMPLES

Ecology words

	1	2	3	4
	soil	water	erosion	conservation

Automotive words

	1	2	3	4
	car	racer	snowmobile	automobile

IV. CONTEXTUAL ANALYSIS

Rationale

Readers of all ages constantly and unconsciously use the context to figure out the meanings of unknown words. Even primary children can read words in sentences which they can't recognize in a list, showing their natural use of the sense of a sentence in word recognition. Contextual clues are numerous. They include the position of the word in a sentence, figures of speech, actual definitions or explanations of a word, appositive phrases or clauses, and the like.

We do not try to teach pupils to look for these structures in a sentence, in the way we teach them to recognize the relationships of the parts of a sentence. In reading, a child uses the contextual clues by thinking out the relationships and by drawing on his experiences with language through listening, speaking, and reading. In other words, he responds to such clues as tone, mood, and synonyms, not because he knows the terms to describe these things, but because he has experienced such sentences before and can guess or feel the meaning. Hence, the goal of our exercises in contextual analysis is to promote thinking about the probable meanings of unfamiliar words, not to convey formal knowledge of their structural characteristics. Any of these exercises will be improved by having children discuss their thinking during the exercise, after they have completed it.

THE CHILD WILL LEARN:

to read an entire sentence before analyzing it for
   the meaning of an unknown word
to react actively to possible clues within a
   sentence
to show increasing skill in deriving word
   meanings from the context
to combine contextual clues with other clues,
   such as phonic, structural, or syllabication clues
to derive the pronunciation of a word from
   contextual clues

IDEA CLUES—INFERENCE, COMPARISON,
AND CONTRAST

187. Before you plan to read a short story to the class, choose a dozen or so words from the story and write them on the board prior to reading the story aloud. Tell the listeners that the words on the board belong in the story, and when you pause in your reading, they are to supply the next word, choosing it from the list. This activity develops listening skills and involves the use of context clues.

188. Select a paragraph or short story from any reading source. Black out every fifth word. Place a number above each blank space to correspond with numbers listed on paper. The students read the story and write the word they think is missing on the corresponding blank. Students will enjoy comparing differences. Stress the point that inserted words must make sense within the context.

John and Sue go _____ every Saturday. They take _____ with them.

1. _____
2. _____

189. *Hint:* New vocabulary should be introduced in the context of a sentence that is within the student's experience.

When your throat tickles, you _____.
(cough)
What sound do you make when your nose tickles? (Sneeze)

190. Write a brief story omitting many of the initial letters of words. Students may also write such stories as an activity in creative writing.

EXAMPLE

Two little ＿oys went for a walk in the ＿oods.
As they walked down the ＿ath, one ＿oy
stopped. He bent down to look at a ＿orm
crawling along the ＿ath. The other ＿oy heard
a noise and looked to see a ＿ird flying from
a ＿ree.

191. Type on spirit masters stories about cowboy life in the old West, about space travel, or about other unit material for review. Omit terms related to the subject. Run off enough sheets for the class. Students read the story and fill in the blanks with the correct terms. This may be done as a game with a small group.

The stories may also be put on acetate sheets and used over and over again.

EXAMPLE

In the old West cowboys lived on the (range,
prairie). *To be sure each rancher knew his own
cattle, he burned his* (brand) *on each cow.
This was done during the spring of the year at*
(roundup) *time. Newborn calves would be*
(lassoed), *then* (branded) *with a hot iron.*

192. Type several paragraphs of a story, but omit every fifth word, leaving a blank space. Students fill in the blanks with words they believe will make the story complete. Discussion should follow, giving attention to words different students used.

193. Have students select five words from the glossary of a book used by the class. They write five sentences, omitting the chosen word in each one. They read the sentences to the group. The other students try to guess the missing words from the context and from previous reading in the book.

194. Sentences and words from the textbook are used to strengthen meaning from the context. These may be done on charts or board, or they may be duplicated. Tell the students to read the sentences and answer the questions on the sheet.

EXAMPLE

The boy walked briskly down the winding path.

1. *Underline the word which tells you how the boy walked.*
2. *Circle the word which tells you the path was not straight.*

195. The child must be trained to use context rather than guesswork to unlock a new word. For practice in this area, write several sentences, leaving out an important word in each one. The new words should be read in context for checking purposes.

EXAMPLE

1. *Be sure to _____ the sentence by putting in the commas and period.* (punctuate)
2. *Mr. Jones's _____ was caused by his recent sickness.* (infirmity)

SENTENCE STRUCTURE—WORD POSITION, FIGURES OF SPEECH, WORD FUNCTIONS, AND PROVERBS

196. The teacher prepares large cards, each bearing one word of a sentence. Each child is given a card. The children then line up so the sentence reads correctly. One child is asked to sit down, and the sentence is reread without the omitted word. This helps children discover the importance of a word to the structure of the sentence. The missing word may even change the meaning of a sentence.

This technique may be used to construct sentences. The cards are given out, and the child who has the first word comes to the front. The child who thinks he has the second word joins him, and they continue until the sentence is correctly constructed.

197. Duplicate a list of sentences in which the words have been arranged in mixed order. The student reads each sentence and underlines the word which would come first when the sentence is in its proper order. Be sure your sentences are pertinent to the children's interests and, if possible, use their names in the sentences. Circle the last word to simplify the task for immature children.

EXAMPLES

went Sue the(zoo)Mother and to.
(outside) to went Bill play.
is(name)your What?

198. Phrases or idiomatic expressions from the text may be written on the overhead projector or duplicated. Students give the meanings either orally or written.

He was "cross as a bear" means _____
"Happy as a lark" means _____

199. Advertisements use figures of speech to sell their products. Collect old magazines and newspapers for use in the classroom. Groups may be appointed to look for metaphors, similes, or personifications within ads. These may be mounted on charts to display the various ways figures of speech can be applied effectively.

200. Try discussing a different proverb each week, for example, "A bird in hand is worth two in the bush." Discussion might follow such questions as: Do you think this saying really refers to birds? What do you think it means? How could it apply to you?

201. Proverbs and titles may be rewritten by the teacher. The students locate the correct answers by using the dictionary. Students are encouraged to rewrite proverbs on their own and have the others guess them.

Proverb: *A stitch in time saves nine.*

Teacher's version: *A small tear repaired immediately will save a large patch later.*

5

Language Development and Vocabulary

I. ORAL COMMUNICATION

Rationale

In ever-increasing numbers, reading specialists are recognizing the relevance of the development of the child's language skills for reading success. Classroom teachers are realizing that learning to read is more than simply saying words in the reader. Children cannot really learn to read, in the sense that reading is thinking with words, unless their own language skills are well developed—in other words, unless they can first use words in meaningful ways. Reading progress is limited when children use baby-talk or substitute one sound for another. It is almost impossible when they cannot mentally frame sentences to express what they wish to say, or when they offer ideas in fragments or rudimentary strings of words. Reading continues to be memorized word-naming, if the structure of the printed sentences or the ideas they offer are more advanced than the child's own language or his idea background.

The reading program must supply the experiences, or ideas, which may be translated into words—the medium of the reading act. Printed words are only symbols for ideas and concepts which, in turn, are familiar or not according to the experiences of the child. Reading words is not an end in itself but is the amalgamation of the reader's thinking or language ability and first-hand experiences with the concepts offered by the author.

THE CHILD WILL LEARN:

to speak largely in complete thoughts or sentences

to be familiar with various patterns of sentences in speech and in printed matter

to vary his inflection or intonation within a sentence in keeping with the purpose of the sentence

to develop a growing stock of ideas (words) based on first-hand experiences

to recognize relationships among the ideas expressed by words

to understand the dialect speech of his teacher and peers

to grow in ability to express his own ideas in various ways in an effort to communicate

COMMUNICATION: GROUP AND
INDIVIDUAL ACTIVITIES

202.   *Hint:*   Always have children read silently before orally, except in a testing situation.

203.   *Hint:*   Children are eager to share personal items from home. An opportunity to talk to a small group in a relaxed situation is beneficial for language development. Often this sharing leads to interesting discussions, and much new information will be a side effect. Do not have young children share with the entire class. Their voices do not carry and other children are inclined not to listen, thus creating an unfavorable situation.

204.   Use a tape recorder to compile a group story. A small group of children gathers around the recorder. One child begins telling a story (original) and talks for two minutes. When his time is up, another child takes up the story, then another, and so on. The last child completes the story with an ending. It is great fun to hear the entire story!

205.   A story containing dialogue may be read like parts in a play. Choose a narrator to read descriptive settings, connecting paragraphs, or incidental dialogue. Other children read various characters' parts.

206.   *Hint:*   To increase vocabulary, students should read selections related to the content of the current unit or story in parallel readers of the same series, other basal readers, or in trade books or literary readers correlated with the basal reader. Then share these related bits of knowledge with the group orally.

207.   Two classes can work up an exchange program. Each week, one student prepares a story to read to another class, and someone from that class prepares to read one to your class. This provides children an opportunity to read aloud before a group of strangers. Each child is given an opportunity to participate.

INTERPRETATION, FLUENCY, AND INFLECTION

208. List sentences on the board that require a variety of expressions. Encourage students to determine how they might say these words to show how they feel, using their voices to show the feeling expressed. Several students could read the same sentence, showing different expressions. If you can, tape this session. Students benefit from hearing how they used their voices to show their feelings.

EXAMPLES

But I don't like that food!
Why did you do that?
David! What are you doing?
I don't feel very well.

209. Choose a simple exclamation, such as "Oh!" Students say the exclamation with the inflection needed to react to the statements below:

Someone stepped on your toe.

You see just what you wanted under the

Christmas tree.

You just heard some surprising news.

We will have school this Saturday.

There will be no school tomorrow.

210.   *Hint:*   There are many sources of stories and poems adaptable to choral reading. Use these sources to develop skills in interpretation, fluency, and inflection. Besides, it's fun!

211.   Without inflection, read dramatic excerpts of conversation from a familiar story. Ask the class whether the characters would have spoken differently—if so, how and why. Then have children read the dialogue using stress and tone of voice to show how the characters felt when they spoke.

212.   In reading a sentence, we break it into parts or phrases, for example, Joe went / into the house / to find Mother. Practice saying words in phrases will help children read more smoothly and quickly. Make a set of flash cards, each showing a group of words naturally phrased together when read aloud, as in the examples. Hold the cards up one at a time. Allow about three seconds, then put the card down and call on someone to tell what the card said. Tell the students to watch carefully, for they will have to make their eyes read quickly.

EXAMPLES

in the tree
down the road
saw them coming
up the stairs

213.   Read a sentence several times, emphasizing a different word each time. Students interpret the change of emphasis as each word is stressed.
Follow-up: Students compose sentences and read them aloud to the small group, using these patterns of emphasis.

This is my *lunch.*
This is *my lunch.*
What are you doing *here?*
What are you doing here?

214. Encourage children to write questions they would like to discuss with the rest of the class. They can put these questions or topics in a box with a slot in the top. To avoid embarrassment and encourage more thought-provoking questions, children leave their names off and disguise their handwriting. During a time set aside for this purpose, questions are drawn from the box. Students offer possible solutions during discussion.

Hint: One or two students may be the secretaries and write these questions and solutions on paper so other children can read them during the week.

Role-playing pantomime may be suggested. The teacher should play a passive role and encourage students to answer each other's questions.

215. Start a "mad box." Students can write any feelings they may have about the teacher, fellow classmates, parents, grades, or other topics and put them in the "mad box." They must not use names or four-letter slang. Students may use a thesaurus to find adjectives to express themselves. This often supplies the child with a healthy outlet for his emotions. Encourage the use of descriptive adjectives and tell how they describe feelings with more impact.

216. Students write expressions in dialect on small word cards. These cards are tacked to a large wall map to show where in our country these expressions are used.

217. Children search the library for books that have many dialect expressions. Miniature bookcovers are made to

ILLUSTRATION 215.

represent the books. These small bookcovers are tacked to a large wall map in the proper location for the dialect used in the book.

218.   Children who read well will probably enjoy reading Uncle Remus stories and practicing the dialect. If they can handle it, have them read to the class.

219.   *Hint:* Try to locate an original version of *Bre'r Rabbit* or other Uncle Remus stories. Thoroughly practice reading it aloud, then read it to the class. Discussion will follow, and many questions will probably be asked about various pronunciations.

II. BUILDING SIGHT AND MEANING VOCABULARY

Rationale

> *It is not a new concept that word recognition is the fundamental basis of all reading development. But this recognition has been interpreted by some to mean word-naming and word-calling, thus losing sight of the fact that words simply represent ideas or ways of*

expressing ideas. Words may be the bricks in the building of reading, but word meanings and relationships are the mortar that holds the bricks together. The learner must realize that words do not have a single meaning or a single function in a sentence. Even apparently simple words are not learned by sheer repetition, particularly in lists or drills in isolation, for often even these simple words have multiple meanings and usages. Nor are words learned solely through reading experience, for their understanding depends upon auditory, vocal, and writing experiences. Words are really a group of ideas associated with a central thought, and their true understanding demands practice in learning relationships among and between ideas (words).

THE CHILD WILL LEARN:

to categorize and classify words according to
their meanings
to distinguish the relationships among
homonyms, synonyms, and antonyms
to deal with the multiple meanings and usage
of words
to broaden and deepen his word associations by
using qualifying and descriptive words

CATEGORIZING AND CLASSIFYING WORDS

220. *Hint:* Check Chapter 4 for additional activities in vocabulary development and enrichment.

221. The children draw or cut out of magazines pictures of pets, food, or other objects. A series of charts is made, each one bearing a different heading, such as "Things We Eat" or "Animals We Like." The children sort and classify the pictures, matching them with the appropriate charts. Instead of making large charts, each child may make a dictionary of classified objects.

222.   The following exercise is written on the board or on a chart. The students look at the first two words in each line, then on a piece of paper list two additional words which belong to the same category. They may use the dictionary or word list in the back of their readers for help.

EXAMPLES

dress   shirt   _____   _____
dog   horse   _____   _____
car   airplane   _____   _____

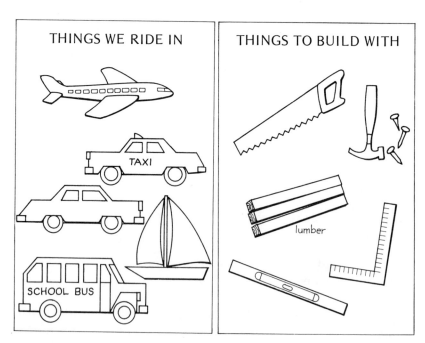

ILLUSTRATION 221.

223. At the top of a sheet of oaktag, print the names or pictures of several kinds of stores (toy store, shoe store, clothing store). Under the name of each store, list some items you could buy there. Cut the lists apart and put the entries in different envelopes. The children try to match the articles with the correct store headings. If desired, the stores and lists could be made from felt or backed with flannel to use on the flannel board.

224. Alphabetizing may be used for many things, including foods. Each player gives the name of a food beginning with a new letter of the alphabet. He names a food starting with *a,* such as *apple;* the next person names one starting with *b,* and so on. Help may be given for letters such as *q, u, x,* or *z.* Quaker oats, quail, upside-down cake, or zucchini may be used.

225. Sheets of paper are labeled by classification headings. Each child maintains his own folder of topics to add to as new words are met in his independent reading. Headings would vary with pupils' work levels. These vocabulary sheets are very helpful during creative writing, to aid in spelling, and to increase descriptive writing.

EXAMPLES

color words	words that describe something
shape words	words for how people feel
family words	words for how people look
ways people can move	words for kinds of talk
	homes for people
doing words	substitutes for people's names
size words	(pronouns)

226. New words from children's experience stories or any reading material are written on small cards, approximately 1×2 inches, one word to a card. The pupil files these alphabetically in a small box. Many activities can be developed using the boxes of words. (*Note:*   Nifty flash cards can be purchased, 1000 per box, 2 × 3 inches, for about a dollar. These cards are excellent for vocabulary games.)

EXAMPLE

During activity period, several students place their a through d words on their desks, word side up. When the leader asks for a category of words, the students hold up their words which apply, reading them aloud when called on. This activity brings about much involvement and helps students to react quickly. Categories from Activity 225 can be used, plus many from other areas of the curriculum: e.g., number words, weather words, animals or transportation.

227.   Use a mail-order catalog for illustrations. Cut out and paste the pictures in a manila folder. Draw lines across the bottom of folder. Strips of stiff paper printed with the names of each item are kept in an envelope stapled to the folder. Students match strips with pictures. An answer card may be kept in the envelope for self-checking. Suggested topics for folders are toys, clothes, tools, animals, round things, square things.

228.   Write words as though you can hear them as well as see them. Think of the sound representation they may convey. For example, the word *slender* may be written with narrow lines to represent meaning. Give the children a feeling for sound representation by having them express words in this creative manner.

229.   On a spirit master, print a list of words that describe *persons, locations,* and *things*. Give the students a code to

CLOTHES

1.	6.
2.	7.
3.	8.
4.	9.
5.	10.

ILLUSTRATION 227.

short

FAT

TALL

WORMY

speedy

ILLUSTRATION 228.

use in marking their paper: person—P, location—L, thing—T. Have students indicate with this code whether each noun is a person, location, or thing.

EXAMPLES

Sally—P	*umbrella—T*
cap—T	*Ohio—L*
Chicago—L	*nickel—T*
brother—P	*John—P*

VARIATION

> *This could be made more difficult by having students indicate why, what, where, and how.*

EXAMPLES

in the house—where	*it was raining—why*
he was afraid—why	*the bell—what*
on the tree—where	*by the gate—where*
in the yard—where	*the dog—what*
by car—how	*went very fast—how*

230. This is a game to encourage children to classify household items. The teacher prepares word cards using the names of items usually found in a house. She distributes these cards, then asks for items found in certain rooms or places. The children put the items called for in a trailer made out of a box. The van may be a toy truck or any suitable container.

231. Ask children to name things that belong in a particular category. Students will think of many additional cate-

ILLUSTRATION 230.

gories. Try to keep each category from becoming too broad. Don't have a list of *food* for instance, as there are too many kinds.

EXAMPLES

Things That Move

Wheels	*Feet*	*Wings*	*Crawl*
bicycle	unicorn	eagles	worms
automobile	colt	insects	snake

Musical Instruments

Keys	*Strings*	*Wind*	*Percussion*
piano	violin	clarinet	drums
organ	cello	recorder	cymbals

Tools

Lifting	*Digging*	*Cutting*	*Grinding*
fork	shovel	knife	peppermill
hoe	spade	saw	garbage disposal

232. Children make large charts (18 × 36) for words concerning subjects that interest them. They may categorize them under headings such as those listed below. These charts may be stapled on wire clotheshangers and hung on a chart rack for easy access. These lists are tremendous boosts for expanding vocabulary in creative writing.

Space words: capsule, orbit, experiments.
Funny words: joke, humorous, comical.
Action words: skip, gallop, ran.
Neighborhood words: streets, buildings,
   upkeep, private property.

233. Give each child a copy of a word list pertaining to a particular classification, but in which the spellings have been scrambled. Allow a limited time for students to unscramble the words and write the correct spelling beside each word. The winner is the one with the most unscrambled words rewritten correctly. For poor spellers, a word list might be supplied.

Types of Shelter

Eskimo home (ilogo):   igloo.

Indian home (ntte):   tent.

Early man's home (vcea):   cave.

City dweller's home (tnemaptar):   apartment.

Traveler's overnight home (letho):   hotel.

HOMONYMS, SYNONYMS, ANTONYMS

234. Give each student a copy of words that have homonyms. Have the class give another spelling and definition for each word.

---

fare	maid
bear	night
plane	piece
sell	write
cent	led

235. Have the children make a list of words that are spelled alike but have several meanings. They may draw or cut pictures from magazines to show the difference in meaning. Examples are shown in Illustration 235.

236. Definitions are given that call for double homonym answers. Students read the definitions and try to figure out the homonym pairs needed to complete the answers.

Response to the bill collector (oh, owe).
Man who delivers letters (male, mail).
Broken window (pain, pane).
Look at ocean (see, sea).
To wander about a city in Italy (roam, Rome).

237. This activity is a particularly meaningful home-work assignment. Teams of two students find as many pairs of

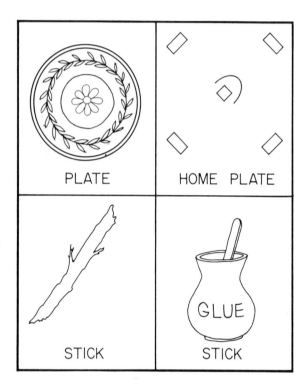

ILLUSTRATION 235.

homonyms as they can from many sources. Each valid pair counts one point. Deduct five points for invalid pairs. For the ground rules, a valid pair is a pair of words that are pronounced alike but spelled differently and have different meanings. Identical phonetic re-spellings in the dictionary would determine like pronunciations. A full week should be given for research. A committee screens the papers to determine the winning team.

238.   *Hint:* Every intermediate-level classroom should have several copies of a good thesaurus. This is an excellent source for obtaining synonyms and antonyms. *Roget's Thesaurus,* in paperback form, is recommended because it is easy to use and inexpensive.

239. Give every child a thesaurus. Then, give challenges, such as "How many synonyms for *fast* can you find?" "How many for *run?*" "How many for *talk?*" "What is the preferred pronunciation of *envelope?*" "How many meanings for the word *joint* can you find?"

240. The child is given a paragraph containing many tired words. The child is asked to replace the tired words with more descriptive words from their readers or reference books, listing them below the original words. Less able students will need a list to choose from.

EXAMPLE

Tom walked *through the woods. He* saw a *squirrel*

strolled	*spied*
sauntered	*noticed*

hurrying *up a tree.*

scampering
scurrying

241. List words that have obvious antonyms and have students think of as many antonyms as they can. The more mature the students' reading skills, the more antonyms they will think of for each word.

This may be done orally or as a written exercise.

EXAMPLES

sweet (sour, bitter)	last (first, initial, beginning)
play	late
new	difficult
short	large

242. Children are seated on the floor in a semi-circle. The teacher, or leader, spins an old 78 rpm phonograph record in the center of the group. As it spins, the leader calls out a word that has an obvious opposite, then calls a child by name. That child must say an opposite and catch the record before it falls flat.

VARIATION

> *Synonyms, homonyms, beginning sounds, or rhymes may be used.*

243. Divide a circular piece of cardboard into twelve pie-shaped sections. In each section write words that are easily recognizable as antonyms. Number each section as in Illustration 243. Up to four players take turns rolling dice. The number they roll tells them which word they must give an opposite for. If a player gives a correct word, he records that number as his score.

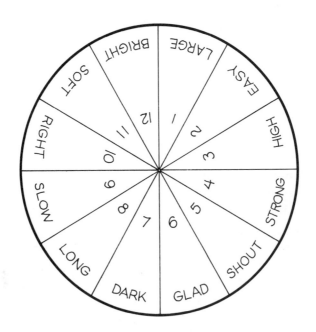

ILLUSTRATION 243.

If he cannot give a correct opposite, he loses that turn. The first player to reach fifty points is winner.

Additional discs with new words may be paper-clipped onto the board so that the vocabulary is different for the next game. Use more difficult vocabulary for upper grades.

244.   Children are encouraged to analyze new words they do not know for pronunciation and meaning. Often this can be very misleading. For example, the word *jailbird* might refer to a bird in prison. List several words whose meanings may be misinterpreted if analyzed part by part. Logical but incorrect meanings may be listed in a second column. Have students match the words with the definitions and describe the logic behind each meaning. Students add new words as they are able.

EXAMPLES

tulips: *a mouth*
exact: *dance done by eggs*
lettuce: *asking permission to do something*
groovy: *deep ridges*
carpetbagger: *one who wraps carpets*

245.   Divide the class into two teams and provide a red tag for one team, a blue tag for the other. Use a playing board similar to a baseball diamond. The game begins with both tags on home plate. The teacher acts as pitcher, giving each player a word which he must pronounce and use in a sentence concerning baseball. If the player uses his word correctly, his team's tag is moved from home to first base. If the next player fails, he is "out" and the first tag remains at its present base. After three "outs" the other team comes to bat. Teams take turns pronouncing and using a word in a sentence. One run is scored each time the team tag rounds the bases and returns to home plate. Suggested words are arrange, supply, fan, gate, magazine.

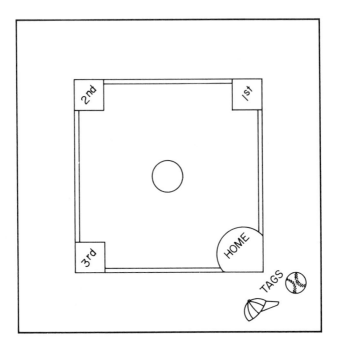

ILLUSTRATION 245.

246. Start the group with a few words that have multiple meanings and origins but are pronounced and spelled alike. Discuss the many meanings orally. Then have the children search throughout the week for additional concepts and patterns of use. At the end of the week, students may bring in their lists for further discussion.

EXAMPLES

*run (speed, stockings, kennel, river, nose,
     election)*
fair (complexion, just, display)
fast (speed, not, eat, secure)
bar (guard against, saloon, solid material)

247. Some words disappear from our vocabulary use as generations pass and technology changes. New words are thought of to fit new products and situations. Students will benefit from a discussion of why words are eliminated and others are added.

EXAMPLES

sneakers   *bloomers*   *leggings*
slip-ons   *mules*   *shay*

VARIATION

Students use their imaginations to dream up new words to fit a product—perhaps a new name for a cereal, a game, or a word to describe how they might feel.

QUALIFYING OR DESCRIPTIVE WORDS

248. Action and descriptive words are introduced with primary children. Sentences are written on the board, omitting the action or descriptive words. Students supply possible insertions. Students discuss the possibilities in the group, then make up a new sentence to work on independently.

EXAMPLE

The _____ car _____ down the street.

old   went
new   bounced
battered   sped

249. Write on chalkboard or transparency, in sequence, such phrases as *the house, the white house, the large white house, the large white house with green shutters.* Encourage students to describe how the addition of each descriptive phrase alters the image of the first phrase.

Follow-up: As an individual activity, give each student a dittoed copy of such undefined phrases as *a boat, the horse, a table,* and *the zoo,* and have him expand each phrase by adding as many descriptive phrases as possible.

250. Students may illustrate something smooth, something soft, something rough, or something pretty. Then they either dictate what is to be written or, if able, write the description. Booklets may be made as an extension activity.

EXAMPLE

Soft: *My pillow is soft. It holds my head.*

251. Students can come up with original ideas for describing intangible terms. Use this activity as a creative writing lesson. Be sure all the students understand what kinds of noun forms qualify as intangibles. Have them see how many original ideas they can think of. Crayon illustrations may also be made for further enrichment. Nouns such as those below may be used.

EXAMPLES

Happiness is _____   Hungry is _____
Love is _____   Tired is _____
Misery is _____   Confusion is _____

252. Students choose a noun from the story they are reading. Write the word across the page, spaced as shown in the example. Then they think of adjectives that will describe the noun, beginning with each letter in the chosen word. Caution students against choosing a word with the same letter used more than once (e.g., *book*).

EXAMPLES

h	*o*	*r*	*s*	*e*
hairy	*old*	*red*	*silky*	*energy*
high	*ornery*	*racy*	*stubborn*	

253. To identify and describe sounds, have students close their eyes while one student performs an action that entails a definite sound, such as sharpening a pencil or knocking on a door. After the sound has been identified, ask the class to suggest words that most accurately describe the sound.

EXAMPLE

Students' descriptive words and phrases of a pencil being sharpened might be:

scratchy	*scraping*
whirring	*grinding*

254. Bring an imaginary box full of presents into the room. Each child pretends to reach into the box, picks a present, unwraps it, and begins describing it to the group. The other children try to guess the imaginary object from the description given.

255. Children form small groups and make a display for the bulletin board. For example, paste one large picture on large cardboard. This can be a picture of an airplane, a teacher, an automobile, a seascape, a landscape, and the like. Ask children to cut out words from magazines that tell something about the picture, such as *fabulous, beautiful, intelligent, good.*

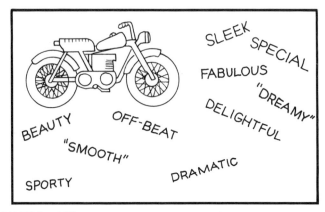

ILLUSTRATION 255.

256. Television commercials and colorful advertisements command children's attention. What is it about advertising methods that attract us so strongly? Discuss this with the group, giving attention to color, arrangement, and descriptive writing. Stress interesting word usage, vivid language, and imagery. Following the discussion, students may write word pictures and advertising jargon to "sell" a favorite product.

257. Discuss the importance of descriptive and action words in evoking definite sensory images. Choose such words from a story the class has just read, for example, *boiling, stormy, winding, hissing*. List them on the board, and have students explain what image each of the words brings to mind.

Encourage children to find other such words in their books and to describe the images each word calls to mind.

EXAMPLES

I feel boiling mad!
The coffee is boiling over!
I was so hot I was boiling.
The rapids were boiling with foam.

258. Ditto a list of action words, numbering them as indicated in the example below. The children write their own sentences in which these words could be used, putting the numerals for the words that fit the sentence in the blanks.

EXAMPLE

1. danced   5. hurried
2. limped   6. raced
3. skipped   7. walked
4. hopped   8. staggered

The boy __5–6__ down the field.
His paw hurt, the dog __2–3–4–8__ to his master.
She was so happy she __1–3–5–6__ down the street.

259. Another way to elicit descriptive words is by having an "Apple Party." Each child brings a small apple to school. Observe the apple and list as many words as possible to describe how it looks, feels, smells, and tastes. The last area, of course, is tasting, as they eat their apples.

EXAMPLES

looks	feels	smells	tastes
red	hard	sweet	sweet
spotted	cold	fresh	juicy
good	round		

VARIATION

Use cookies, grapes, candy.

Hint: For additional activities that may be useful in vocabulary enrichment, see Chapter 6.

6

Location
Skills

Rationale

Although it is often lost sight of in the reading program, our greatest goal is to produce independent readers—individuals who can use reading for their own life purposes. Independence in reading demands skill in using books and other resource materials. Among the most frequently used resources are the dictionary and the library, and development of skill in their use is an essential part of the reading program.

Many pupils never learn to use the dictionary for any other value than the meaning of a difficult word. They fail to attend to the information given regarding pronunciation, derivation, or usage. Because of this lack, they often fail to retain meanings of words, and the dictionary becomes simply a momen-

tary aid. Many of the library skills that must be learned are quite mechanical, and their practice is often divorced from actual library use. For these reasons, many pupils never realize the values of a library and seldom use it after leaving school.

Excellent, interesting reference materials, such as a thesaurus, the World Almanac, pamphlets, government publications, catalogs, and newspapers lie virtually untouched in many classrooms and libraries.

We have tried to recognize some of these instructional deficiencies in outlining activities in these areas. But the task of making this learning functional depends on the teacher's skill in presenting the materials in an interesting and understandable way. Whenever possible, these activities should include actual use of the suggested resource materials.

THE CHILD WILL LEARN:

to use the alphabetic arrangement of the
   dictionary
to use guide words
to interpret the pronunciation key
to derive meanings suited to context for
   difficult words
to understand usage terms and abbreviations
to use aids in a book, such as the index, table
   of contents, glossary
to employ the card catalog in finding books
to become familiar with various resource and
   reference materials
to use telephone directories as resource material

I. DICTIONARY SKILLS

ALPHABETIC SEQUENCE

260.   Use the individual card holders (Activity 461) or the large pocket holder for flash cards to arrange letters in alphabetical order. Small cards are made for each letter. Also make small cards that begin with each letter and that include a picture of something beginning with that letter. (It should be obvious what the picture is.) Each letter, with a picture, is placed in sequence in the card holder.

Two students play a game, taking turns calling out a letter. The other player must pull out the letter and the picture and name both. No score is kept—they just take turns and help each other when needed.

261.   Promote vocabulary development by challenging students to organize words according to alphabetical order. Using any story they are presently reading, they locate words beginning with each letter. Since each child may be read-

ILLUSTRATION 260.

ing a different story, this is a difficult activity to check, but not every task needs to be checked—it's just fun to do them!

262. Prepare several packs of 3 × 5 word cards, five words to a pack. Give each player a pack of cards. At the teacher's signal, every player arranges his word cards alphabetically. The first one to complete the task correctly scores five points, the second to finish scores four points, and so forth. Each player tallies his own score.

When one round has been completed, each player passes his group of word cards to the child on his right. The cards are shuffled, and when the signal is given, each player arranges the new group into alphabetical order. The game continues until each player has used every group of word cards. The player with the highest score is the winner.

EXAMPLE

Sample word card groups:
Group 1:   barn, road, church, window, party.
Group 2:   field, dirt, baby, lake, kitchen.

263. Make a game board, as shown in Illustration 263, from a square of plastic, oilcloth or cardboard. Write a series of three letters in each section. When children are ready to play, place a spinner in the center. Each child takes turns spinning, then says the series in proper alphabetical order.

As skill increases, make each series longer. Correct sequence may be marked on the reverse side of the game board.

264. Secret messages are an effective and pleasant means of practicing alphabet sequence. On the board write a message in secret code. Use simple codes, such as the next letter in the alphabet in place of the desired letter, or the number of

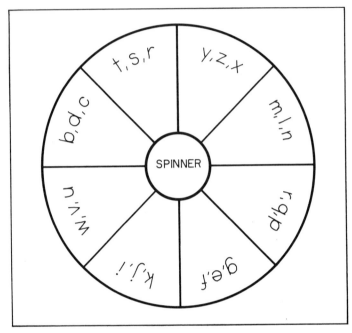

ILLUSTRATION 263.

the letter as it appears in the alphabet. The students decipher
the code, then follow the directions of the message.

<table>
<tr><td>s</td><td>b</td><td>j</td><td>t</td><td>f</td><td>z</td><td>p</td><td>v</td><td>s</td><td>i</td><td>b</td><td>o</td><td>e</td><td rowspan="2">"Raise Your Hand"</td></tr>
<tr><td>18</td><td>1</td><td>9</td><td>19</td><td>5</td><td>25</td><td>15</td><td>21</td><td>18</td><td>8</td><td>1</td><td>14</td><td>4</td></tr>
</table>

265. List words on the board taken from the dictionary. Have students locate each word and write the words that
precede and follow the given word in the dictionary.

266. On the board, specify categories such as countries, foods, and animals. Students copy the headings and, under
each one, list items beginning with different letters of the alphabet. Words should be written in alphabetic sequence.

COUNTRIES	FOODS	ANIMALS
Austria	apple	ant
Belgium	butter	baboon
Cuba	cantaloupe	cow

267. Students try to find words beginning with each letter of the alphabet that fit into each classification written on the board. Many resource books can be used, such as an almanac, dictionary, story books.

SPACE	FAMOUS PEOPLE IN SPORTS	TRANSPORTATION
air	Arnold Palmer	automobile
belt	Babe Ruth	bus

ALPHABETIZING BY FIRST,
SECOND, THIRD LETTERS

268. The names of the characters in a story may be used as an exercise in alphabetical order. Have students alphabetize the names by first names, and again by last names (if given).

Adam
Archie
Betty
José
Karl

269. A room telephone directory may be compiled by a small group or the entire class. Be sure to have parents' permission to include their child's number in the class directory. Each child's name is listed in alphabetical order. Check for correct spelling. Every telephone number must be entered precisely and neatly. Due to the careful listing and copy work required, this activity may be used with a remedial group. The pupils may use carbon paper and make copies for each member of the class. A room directory of names and addresses may be made at Christmas or Valentine's Day for reference by the pupils.

270. Duplicate the following activity on a spirit master and distribute. Discuss the directions with students and assist them in locating at least one item. Students are taught to quickly locate a listing in the Yellow Pages using guide words. Guide words are usually the first three letters of the first and last listings on the page. For example, if the first listing is *motorcycles* and the last listing is *movers,* the guide words might be *MOT–MOV.* Guide words are usually found in the upper left corner of the page.

EXAMPLE

Instruct students to locate these items in the Yellow Pages and to write the guide words for the page on which the items are found.

Housecleaning _____	Engravers _____
Goldfish _____	Picture framing _____
Farm supplies _____	Radio stations _____
Auction Houses _____	Window washers _____
Car wash _____	Cemetery plots _____
Bicycle repairs _____	Music lessons _____
Schools _____	Bus stations _____
Upholsterers _____	Stamp collectors _____

271. The general listing, or white pages, also uses guide words. Students can use the guide words to locate several friends' names and telephone numbers. They should record the guide words for each listing.

Name	*Number*	*Guide Words*

272. To motivate interest in guide words, students can make an attractive bulletin board display, such as that in Illustration 272.

273. Use a regular flash card chart for practicing the use of guide words. Students place the guide words on the left and right sides of the chart. Make additional word cards that are to be placed between the proper guide words. Word cards may be kept in the bottom slot as shown in Illustration 273. A self-checking card may be placed in the number 2 pocket.

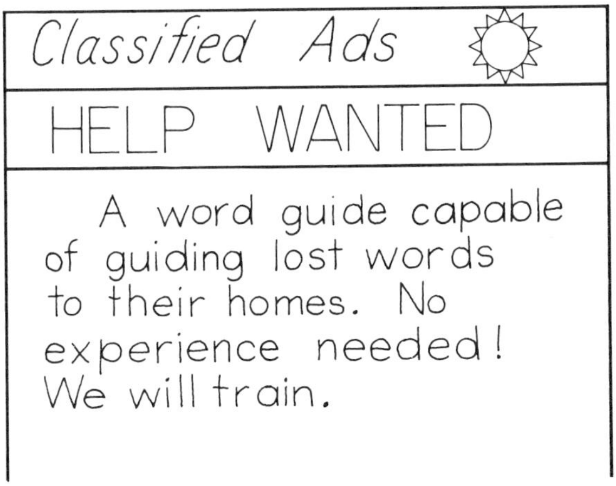

Classified Ads ☼

HELP WANTED

A word guide capable of guiding lost words to their homes. No experience needed! We will train.

ILLUSTRATION 272.

```
┌─────────────────────────────────────────────┐
│  GUIDE      POCKETS        GUIDE              │
│  WORDS                     WORDS             │
│ ┌──────┐  ┌──────────┐   ┌───────┐           │
│ │ ape  │  │ basket   │   │ cute  │           │
│ └──────┘  └──────────┘   └───────┘           │
│ ┌──────┐  ┌──────────┐   ┌───────┐           │
│ │dance │  │ elephant │   │ frost │           │
│ └──────┘  └──────────┘   └───────┘           │
│ ┌──────┐  ┌──────────┐   ┌───────┐           │
│ │ game │  │ ground   │   │ igloo │           │
│ └──────┘  └──────────┘   └───────┘           │
│ ┌──────┐                 ┌───────┐           │
│ │ jam  │                 │ lemon │           │
│ └──────┘                 └───────┘           │
│ ┌──────┐                 ┌───────┐           │
│ │market│                 │ open  │           │
│ └──────┘                 └───────┘           │
│ ┌──────┐                 ┌───────┐           │
│ │pencil│                 │ rabbit│           │
│ └──────┘                 └───────┘           │
│ ┌──────┐                 ┌───────┐           │
│ │ same │                 │ ugly  │           │
│ └──────┘                 └───────┘           │
│ ┌──┐       ┌──┐           ┌──┐                │
│ │  │       │  │           │  │                │
│ ├──┴───────┼──┴───────────┼──┴──────────┐     │
│    1            2              3              │
└─────────────────────────────────────────────┘
```

ILLUSTRATION 273.

ABILITY TO INTERPRET
PRONUNCIATION KEY

274. Divide the class into teams. Provide a dictionary for each student. Write a word on the chalkboard. Signal the teams to open their dictionaries, find the word, and pronounce it correctly. The first student to do so wins a point for his team.

275. Using the International Phonetic Alphabet, the student writes a short story or a note to a friend. This alphabet may be found in most dictionaries.

aɪ dʒəˈmt ovər ʒˈɵ dits ˈkæn jiu?

ABILITY TO TRY SEVERAL DEFINITIONS
IN CONTEXT

276. Give students ditto sheets with several sentences on them. Be sure each sentence contains words with multiple meanings. Underline these words. Students check the dictionary to determine which number definition is used for each word. He writes the number above each one for checking purposes.

2
The boy received a <u>letter</u> saying he had won a
6
<u>letter</u> in football.
16   1
The boy <u>drew</u> a picture of a dining <u>table</u>.

277. Give each student a ditto sheet containing several sentence groups. Each group should contain three sentences, with one word underlined in each. In two of the sentences the word has the same meaning, while in the other it has a different one. Students indicate the two sentences with the same meaning by putting a check in front of them.

_____ Mother taught me to <u>drive</u> the car.
_____ How far can you <u>drive</u> a golf ball?
_____ Will you <u>drive</u> me to the store?

278.   Several players make a list of five or more words they believe their opponents will not know the meaning of. They define their words three ways: one correct meaning, and two incorrect meanings.

When it is a player's turn, he says a word, giving all three meanings. Opponents vote as to which is correct. The player gets 3 points if they choose an incorrect definition and no points if they choose the correct definition.

279.   Write approximately fifteen scrambled words on the board with the dictionary page numbers where the words can be found. Each child is given a dictionary and a sheet of paper. He uses the dictionary to find the words that are scrambled, then writes the words in meaningful sentences.

VARIATION

> *Each student writes an original story using all the words on the list. Then they compare their stories to see how different the stories can be even though the same words were used.*

                                                            EXAMPLES

ewrid, p. _____ (weird)   *ganry, p.* _____ (angry)
ttnoco, p. _____ (cotton)   *yghnur, p.* _____ (hungry)

280.   Involve math, social studies or science along with a sense of fun in learning to use the dictionary.

1. *Find the combined lengths of a vole, a walrus and a newborn alligator.*
2. *Which is largest: crickets, centipedes, or inch-worms?*
3. *Which would you enjoy for dessert: trifle, stroganoff, or mush?*
4. *If you were going fishing, would you take: a fly, a velocipede, or a leader?*
5. *If you lived in Scotland, would you wear brogans, a serape, or a sporan?*

281. Write on the chalkboard the words *mouth, eyes,* and *feet* as labels for three columns. On the side of the board, write a list of descriptive verbs, such as *lope, warble, sashay, peruse, vocalize, scrutinize,* and *harangue.* Ask students whether, for example, one *lopes* with his mouth, eyes, or feet. Then, have children locate each word in the dictionary, read all the definitions given, and determine which category the word belongs in.

EXAMPLE

mouth	eyes	feet
warble	scrutinize	lope

282. Make a spirit master with the following activity: If someone gave you a *yurt,* would you *eat* it, *wear* it, or *live in* it? Ask yourself what you would do with each of the items below. Then write each word under the heading you think is the right one. Afterward, check the words you are not really sure of with your dictionary. You may find that you would have done some very strange things!

Later, make a worksheet, with different headings and words, to trade with someone. Use your dictionary to find tricky words.

yogurt	chorizo	sari	weskit
dormitory	yurt	scow	sanctuary
camisole	cutlet	brogan	loafer
marrow	hovel	tam	zucchini
herbs	abode	frock	garb
alcove	venison	game	mollusk
veal	leotard	frigate	vestibule
drawers	fedora	mules	quarters
domicile	lair	diggings	tapioca
rarebit	pasta	farina	cummerbund
Eat it?		*Wear it?*	*Live in it?*

283. Dictionary code. Intermediate students enjoy codes and ciphers. Using the same dictionary that is used for class work, write a simple sentence in code on the board, or duplicate copies of several sentences that will pique their curiosity. Students could write notes to classmates in code, putting the dictionary to interesting use. Students may volunteer to put messages on the board on their assigned days.

EXAMPLE

1	2	3
718	2	5
326	1	3
83	1	1
442	1	2
116	2	6

Column 1 refers to the page in the dictionary
Column 2 refers to the column on that page
Column 3 refers to number of entries down that
    column

This code reads, "Who has a new baby?"

The Thorndike-Barnhart Beginning Dictionary (Scott-Foresman, Inc.) is recommended for this exercise.

ABBREVIATIONS

284. A committee of students can make an abbreviation booklet. Pages included might be:

        states
        streets
        linear measure
        occupations
        days
        months
        time
        businesses

285. To review state abbreviations, make up clues to remind students of certain abbreviations. The clues may be duplicated and given to each player in the group. Have the players write the correct responses and suggested abbreviations, or two players may orally quiz each other. Each correct answer counts one point, and the player with the most points wins.

EXAMPLES

The vessel in which Noah and his family sailed.
(ark, Ark.)

Pro is for something, _____ is against.
(con, Conn.)

A medical doctor is called an _____.
(MD, Md.)

286. Sometimes students do not realize that nicknames are often abbreviations. Make a bulletin board display where students can match nicknames with the original names. Students will think of many additions to the examples in Illustration 286.

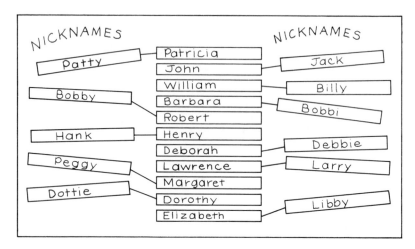

ILLUSTRATION 286.

Library Skills

CARD CATALOG

287. Each student chooses a special topic of interest. He checks the card catalog to see how many books are available in the school library on his chosen topic.

288. In the Teacher's Guide of your basal reader, you will probably find lists of book titles for further reading. Allow a committee of students to take the list to the library. They check the card catalog to see which of the recommended titles are available. They can check out the books for the class.

289. When a student enjoys a book by a particular author, suggest that he check the Author Index in the card catalog to see what other books may be available by that author.

REFERENCE BOOKS

290. Direct students' attention to words of similar visual detail but of very different meanings, as *accept, except;*

went, want; from, form; prescribe, subscribe. Ask students to list other groups of words which at a glance appear alike but have different spellings and definitions.

Follow-up: Give each child a copy of sentences, such as those below, and have him cross out the incorrect word and write the proper one in the blank.

EXAMPLES

The whether map predicted a storm. _____
My mother prescribes to several magazines. _____
She excepted the invitation to my party. _____

291. Have each student pretend he is a travel agent and "sell" the class on visiting a city or vacation area on their vacations. The *World Almanac* and travel folders and magazines are excellent sources of information.

292. Give these instructions on dittoed sheets to your students:

The *World Almanac* is a treasurehouse of interesting facts. Reading it is like eating potato chips—once you begin, it is hard to stop. There is so much information that we really need to use the index. Use the index of a *World Almanac* to locate the page numbers where you could find out about:

	page
The number of bicycle accidents	_____
Information about the Alamo	_____
Awards to actors and actresses	_____
Pay scale of the U.S. Army	_____
Little League baseball	_____
Facts about volcanoes	_____
World's longest tunnel	_____

293.   Try out the "Thinkbox" in Illustration 293 to see how many words students can think of that will fit in each column. Notice that all items in a column must begin with the letter shown and must also belong under that heading. When they are stumped, use the *World Almanac* for aid.

294.   The *World Almanac* has interesting information on famous museums and churches. Have individuals share with the class the one they would like to visit and why.

295.   The *World Almanac* lists interesting biographical facts about the U. S. presidents and their wives. Ask indi-

Animals	Cities	Nations	Rivers	Famous People
T	H	I	N	K

Games	Tools	Automobiles	Clothes	Authors
F	A	C	T	S

ILLUSTRATION 293.

viduals or small groups to tell the class about a president and his wife.

296. The *World Almanac* is an excellent source for individual or small-group research projects. Ask students to share with the class short, interesting verbal reports on the following:

> *How to get a U. S. passport.*
>
> *How to get a patent for an invention.*
>
> *How to get a copyright for literary, musical, or artistic work.*
>
> *How to become an American citizen.*

297. Each student is assigned (or draws from a box) a city somewhere in an area the class is studying. Using a good encyclopedia, they locate information about their cities, such as the list below. Children will add to the list of topics for research.

> *How would I get there? Routes?*
>
> *How far is it from here?*
>
> *What is the climate?*
>
> *Population.*
>
> *Types of industry.*

298. Make a word puzzle using clues concerning information about famous mountain peaks, countries, or rivers. Divide the group into pairs of partners, and provide reference material such as geography books, the *World Almanac,* and the atlas. The teams use the reference books in completing the puzzle. Clues will pertain to the subject being studied. The sample questions below should be expanded to cover other interests and information.

EXAMPLE (mountains)

1. *Highest peak in the United States.*
2. *Explorer had this peak named for him.*
3. *Highest peak in Oregon.*
4. *Famous heads carved in mountain.*

PROJECTS IN FINDING RESOURCE
MATERIALS FOR REPORTS

299. *Hint:* Use recordings, films, filmstrips, and other related materials as listed in the Teacher's Guides that accompany your basal readers and other tests to enrich the child's background for each unit or story. Do not neglect the search through available catalogs and lists provided by publishers.

300. Children who are sports fans may make a bulletin board display with newspaper or magazine clippings. Local, college, or pro teams may be used. Lists of team or indi-

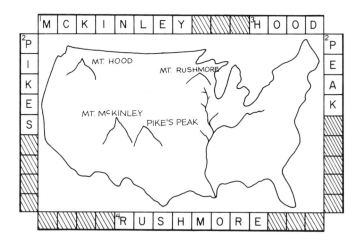

ILLUSTRATION 298.

vidual statistics should be compiled and changed weekly as the season progresses.

301. A small group of children work on a class mural. Information learned in a science, social studies, reading, or health unit may be displayed in mural form. A committee screens ideas and assigns objects or space on the mural. Encourage students to use a wide variety of textured material, such as cloth, cotton, trim, or wallpaper.

302. Small groups use current events to set up a news program. One student, playing "anchor man," summarizes the news, making use of maps, drawings, photographs, or other visual aids in his presentation. "Correspondents" report situations in foreign countries, such as floods, elections, riots, or hijackings. A different news team reports weekly.

303. Allow students to examine the list of available filmstrips in your library. They will learn a great deal by previewing filmstrips and choosing appropriate films for reports in class.

304. On a chart, list questions which arise in class discussions. Have the students locate information on subjects which particularly interest them. Students and the teacher may gather pictures and printed material from information sources. During small group discussions, the information, pictures, and related books may be shared. The collected information may also be organized and arranged as a bulletin board display.

305. *Hint:* Your school library probably has a pamphlet and picture file. Students should have instruction in the kinds of information available in these files and how to make use of this valuable resource aid.

USING TELEPHONE DIRECTORIES

306. Children enjoy compiling a class telephone directory. Each child writes his correct listing as it should appear in the directory. A committee compiles the information ready for duplication. Each child designs his own directory cover.

EXAMPLE

Adams, Carrie L.   4163 Beach Rd.   924–6894

307. Telephone numbers that may be needed in emergencies should be near each person's telephone. Each student can locate the numbers to call and make an attractive chart for his home.

308. Which names appear most in the telephone directory? List the most common names and the number of listings for each.

	name	no. of listings
1.	_____	_____
2.	_____	_____
3.	_____	_____

309. The Yellow Pages of the telephone directory are a useful source for learning about comparative sizes of objects. Turn to any page listing a variety of products. These products can be listed from the largest to the smallest.

310. Old telephone books may provide a unique teaching experience for children. Collect last year's directories, and make a list of names to be found in them. These names may

Help   Ouch!

POLICE _____

SHERIFF _____

AMBULANCE _____   I'M LOST!

FIRE _____

HOSPITAL _____

POISON CLINIC _____

Emergency   Poison

ILLUSTRATION 307.

be listed on the board or on a ditto sheet. The class looks up each name and records the code for that name, for instance: Smith, Robert P.:   35–3–18 (35 = page, 3 = column, 18 = number of entry in the column).

VARIATION

> *The teacher may supply the code and have the class look up the names and alphabetize them.*

311.   Advertisers in the Yellow Pages often display an emblem or picture to illustrate their trade. These may be cut from the directory and used for an interesting display. Labels may be kept in an envelope for individuals to match them with the emblems.

312.   Some odd occupations and businesses are listed in the Yellow Pages. Intermediate-level students enjoy locating and discussing these occupations.

EXAMPLES

junk dealers   ditch diggers
flea markets   pet cemeteries

313. Have students choose a business from the Yellow Pages of a telephone directory. List words that "sell or entice" the buyer. Emphasize and discuss the power of descriptive words.

314. An exercise in using guide words in the Yellow Pages of the telephone directory offers students knowledge of how and where to find services.

EXAMPLE

List the guide words to locate the following items:

ITEMS	GUIDE WORDS
Motorcycle	MOT–MOV
House cleaning	HOU–ICE
Goldfish	PET–PHA

315. Students list several types of businesses from the Yellow Pages. Next, list three individual businesses in each category. Use a local city map to locate the business in each list that is closest to school or home.

316. Using a telephone book, have students pick out a career from the Yellow Pages: dry cleaner, attorney, printer, and so on. Using other resource materials, students can:

1. *Write a paragraph describing the chosen career.*

    2.   *Interview someone who is involved in this work.*

    3.   *Inquire as to the need in the community for that career.*

EXAMPLE

How many lawyers, doctors, dry cleaners does a community need per capita? How does this figure compare with the listings (in that field) in the Yellow Pages? (Ask the Chamber of Commerce or ask the businesses that exist.) Are there enough?

317. Have students choose one type of business in the Yellow Pages. Ask them to make a list of words that describe services and products.

EXAMPLE

Insurance
(Products)
a. *Automobile*   c. *Life*
b. *Burglary*   d. *Marine*

(Services)
1. *Protection*
2. *Savings*
3. *Low cost*

318. Doctors are listed in the Yellow Pages under *physicians.* Committees can find out how many different kinds of doctors are listed and what illnesses they actually treat within their specialties. This activity can really develop into an exciting and useful unit of study.

7

Content Reading Skills

Rationale

As the pupil enters the study of the content fields, his reading rapidly expands beyond the simple interpretation of story-type material. Many graphic and visual aids appear in his textbooks and demand a different approach than word-by-word or line-by-line reading. Basic reading skills make almost no contribution to handling these new media. Research on children's development of these content reading skills is not encouraging, for it indicates that many pupils cannot interpret this illustrative material.

Ideally, the child would be given special instruction and help by the teacher every time she used a content textbook with a group. She would be pointing out similarities and differences among graphs,

*maps, charts, and globes and would be teaching chil-
dren how to read and interpret them while they are in
actual use during the lesson. But surveys of teacher
practices show that this approach is not common, for
the teacher has often not been trained in the relevant
reading techniques. She is more apt to depend on
exercises in workbooks than on directed practice in
the situations and materials present in the classroom.*

THE CHILD WILL LEARN:

to find cardinal and general directions on a map
to locate places on maps and globes
to read map symbols and keys
to compare map projections
to make and use charts, graphs, and time lines
to make and interpret simple tables

I. MAP AND GLOBE SKILLS

ABILITY TO ORIENT ONESELF IN
RELATION TO THE CLASSROOM,
SCHOOL, AND COMMUNITY

319. *Hint:* Have an instructional session with the group on how to open and fold maps properly.

320. *Hint:* Collect an assortment of maps to be kept in an accessible spot for students to use. You will need multiple copies of most maps.

Local city map
State map
Vacation spot maps
Regional maps (e.g., southeastern U. S.)
Maps of world, Europe, Asia, other continents

321.   A group of children make a map of their neighborhood, community, or school. Hold a discussion of scale and symbols. Let the children decide on a scale and appropriate symbols to use, and draw the map accordingly. Practice may be given in locating streets, buildings, parks, rivers, and distances from one location to another.

322.   Students can make a large map of their school on butcher paper. Before making a map of the school location, take a walk with students to point out general shapes and wings of classrooms, the cafeteria, the library, and office facilities. Location of trees, play areas, streets, and other familiar landmarks should be discussed.

323.   Students should make a detailed map of the school neighborhood, with streets, parks, homes, buildings, and other features included. Ask a child to tell things he would see on the way to school or going to a designated store. Call attention to safe routes to school and other destinations. The amount of detail should vary according to the age of the child.

324.   A mural, individual drawings, or a sandbox display may be used in making a community map to show areas near the school. Discuss symbols and scales to determine the ones to be used.

325.   Furnish several maps of the local community. Small groups of students locate and mark the routes of different buses (school, city, and others). A different color is used to distinguish each route. For more advanced students, symbols may be used for various stops. Pupils may become very involved in research required to make delivery routes of local services.

LOCATING PLACES ON MAPS AND GLOBES

326. Ask a child to tell about the most interesting place he has visited outside his own community and how he got there. For young children, the teacher records the stories and prints them on charts for the children to read later. A community map may be used to show the route taken. The means of transportation may also be discussed. With older children, trips outside the city or state may be used and routes traced on road maps.

327. Attach a list of questions to a copy of your state map. Place it in a learning center as an activity in map reading.

EXAMPLES

1. *Find our town on the map.*
2. *How far is our town from the state capital?*
3. *Name the states that touch our state.*

328. Collect simple layouts or maps of places, such as Silver Springs, Six Gun Territory, or Disneyland, and have the students make up imaginary tours to various exhibits. Familiarize students with directions, symbols, and other pertinent factors.

329. Have students identify vacation spots or other locations on a map by listing latitudes and longitudes. Each student may list latitudes and longitudes and have other students try to locate his designated area. A state map may be used first, then as skill develops, extend the area.

EXAMPLE

Longitude 118 ° Latitude 34 ° (Disneyland, Calif.)

330. Various maps or outlines are given out. Have the students locate cities, rivers, products, mountains, and other features, or have them color and label designated areas.

331. This activity should be planned to cover several days of involvement. Political–physical world maps or globes may be used to give pupils practice in locating names and places. Each pupil takes a letter in the alphabet and lists the names of physical and political features that begin with that letter. For example, a list for the letter *A* could include Africa, Asia, Amazon river, Amsterdam, Atlas mountains. The person who has the longest correct list at the end of the time limit is the winner.

332. After the class has been exposed to the eight main compass points, they draw maps of camp sites, state parks, or their neighborhood. They make up stories, using map directions to explain the incidents involved. Other students follow the directions to locate the places referred to in the stories.

READING A MAP ACCORDING TO
CARDINAL DIRECTIONS

333. Draw a simple intersection on the board, indicating cardinal directions (north, south, east, west). Below the intersection, write directions for students to follow. Students draw the intersection and the items listed in the directions. The number and difficulty of directions will depend on the skill of your group.

---

1. *A traffic light is in the center of the intersection.*

2. *There is a vacant lot on the NW corner. Write the word* lot *on this corner.*

3. *Filling stations are located on both the SW and SE corners. Draw squares to indicate their locations.*

334. Draw a large intersection on a spirit master. Show the locations of various buildings, homes, playgrounds, and other features. Under the map, list several questions which can be answered by reading the map. Have the pupils complete the questions with short word answers. Check the answers together by having pupils locate the places on the map.

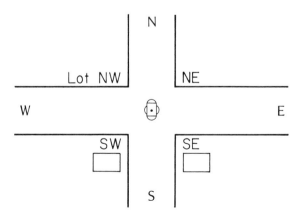

ILLUSTRATION 333.

1. Who is Dick's neighbor?
2. Does Dick live N or S of Nancy?
3. On which street does the church face?
4. Who lives closest to the school?
5. What is across the street from Mike's house?
6. Draw a fire hydrant near the school.

335. In late August and September there are likely to be tropical storms reported on the news. Procure a hurricane map from your local newspaper or radio station. Students delight in listening to the weather report and tracking the storm. This gives excellent practice in using latitude and longitude, in listening skills, and in following directions.

336. *Hint:* To acquaint children with the various scales of miles used on maps, have them examine geography books, encyclopedias, and loose maps. Differences in scales and

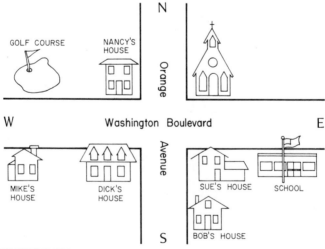

ILLUSTRATION 334.

symbols should be pointed out. Help students realize that maps serve various purposes. They should see and become acquainted with numerous types, not just road maps. Some types to discuss are maps for weather, agriculture, climate, forest, air routes, navigation, solar, and political maps. At the primary level, emphasize awareness of various kinds of maps rather than instruction in reading them. Symbols are also necessary for map reading and understanding. The simplest ones may be illustrated on charts and discussed. Students should also become familiar with basic map colors and what they represent—blue for water, green for forests, black for railroads, and yellow for buildings.

337.   Collect weather maps from newspapers. Mount these on tagboard. The teacher makes statements about a map either orally or in written form. Students interpret the map and respond with "true," "not true," or "I can't tell."

EXAMPLES

*Children in New York must wear coats
    today.*   _____
It is cloudy somewhere in the country.   _____
It is raining somewhere in the southwest. _____
*It is a good day for boating on the nearest
    coast.*   _____
*A high pressure area is moving in from the
    east.*   _____

338.   Give an outline map of an area to a small group of students. Number several places on the map. List the cities, rivers, mountains, and other features to which these numbers refer. Allow each pupil time to refer to other maps and globes, then have them write the correct names by the corresponding numbers. The student with the most correct answers wins.

II. READING GRAPHS AND CHARTS

USING AND MAKING CIRCLE GRAPHS
AND BAR GRAPHS

339. After gaining sufficient knowledge of the compass and protractor, students may make a circle graph of how they spend their time in a twenty-four-hour period. They may also make a pictorial chart.

Time allotments might include: sleeping, eating, odd jobs, outdoor play, indoor play, time at school, and transportation.

340. Measure each child and mark his height on a wall or bulletin board. Indicate each child's name. Encourage pupils to make comparisons as to who is shorter or taller, or how

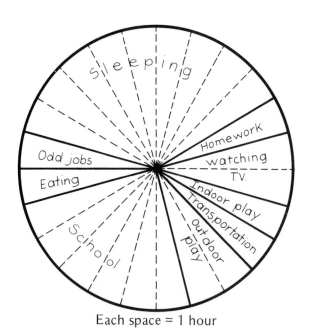

Each space = 1 hour

ILLUSTRATION 339.

many are of the same height. Comparisons may be recorded as a pictorial graph, or the results may be written as a class story chart.

341. Each student may make a graph to show his test scores. Another exercise may be to make a chart or table showing the class average in a certain area.

342. After introducing the concepts of circle graphs, it would be fun for the student to make his own circle graph depicting the allotment of his time during a school day.

Note: In discussion, the students should decide which categories would be best for their particular class situation.

343. Facts and figures are gathered by the students. They compile them to make charts and graphs to accompany

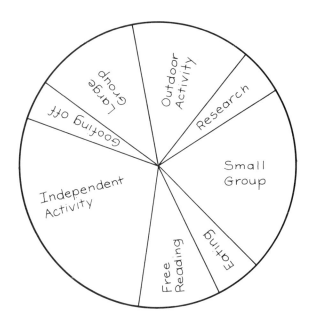

ILLUSTRATION 342.

reports. Students should be encouraged to draw maps or make tables to show information.

344.   Make a survey of the class to see what kinds of soap (or any other commodity) they use. Teams of three or four children may survey different items. Each team member makes a different kind of graph to illustrate their findings.

345.   After graphs have been introduced, give students the experience of collecting and recording data and making their own charts or graphs. Divide the class into teams. Since most children have a pet of some kind, this is a good category to use. With younger children, you may work up the basic graph together. Use categories of cats, dogs, fish, birds, and other animals. Have each team appoint one person to be spokesman, one to count the responses, and one to record the informa-

MARKET RESEARCH

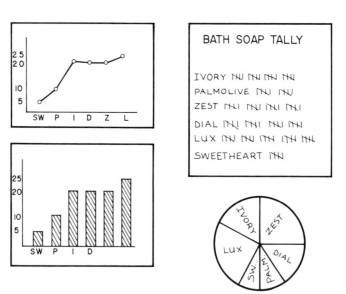

ILLUSTRATION 344.

tion on paper. Make arrangements with other classes for the teams to visit and record information—one team to a room. The teams visit the designated rooms and inquire as to the number of pets each child has. As the questions are asked by the spokesman, one child counts the responses, and another child records the information. After each team returns to their own room, they make a graph to depict the data they collected. The graphs may be displayed in the room and compared by the class.

346. Students can check the newspaper for the daily weather report. A bulletin board or large chart makes a useful display area for daily information. A different child each day has a turn to indicate (1) sunrise, (2) sunset, (3) temperature—low or high or both. The thermometer is made from white cardboard, numbered with degrees. The "mercury" is a piece of red and a piece of white ribbon, sewed together and pulled through vertical slits cut in the top and bottom of the thermometer, to indicate temperature. Movable hands on the cardboard clocks indicate times of sunrise and sunset.

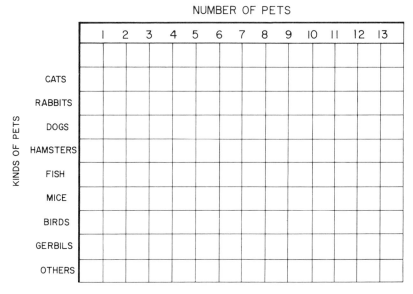

ILLUSTRATION 345.

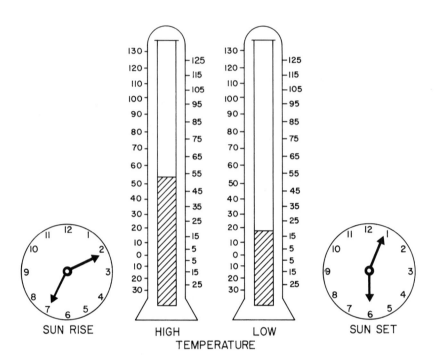

ILLUSTRATION 346.

VARIATION

> *Older children may want to add devices for wind speed and rainfall.*

III. READING TABLES

INTERPRETING AND MAKING SIMPLE
TABLES FROM COMMON SOURCES

347. *Hint:* The *World Almanac* is a classroom essential. It includes tables of virtually every description and category. Activities in this area may center around locating and interpreting information on population, consumption of goods, imports and exports, and other categories.

348. A child planning an actual trip may provide just the incentive needed to create interest. Help plan the time of departure, length of the trip, and time of arrival by consulting a timetable. Information may also be gathered about the city to be visited.

349. Following the reading of a story or a book containing events that occur over an extended period of time, students benefit from making a time line involving the events in the order of their occurrence. This may be done with printed material telling the events and dates, accompanied by student illustrations or cutouts from commercial sources.

350. If you live in a coastal area, students can check the newspaper for the table that lists high and low tides. The table often lists information for several consecutive days. Students can note the time lapse between high tides yesterday, today, and tomorrow.

351. A timetable may be made from tagboard. Students record the time and stops involved in getting to and from school or other places in the community. If children arrive by school bus, an interesting chart can be made showing different bus routes and names of children who ride each bus.

352. Collect timetables for local transportation services, such as city buses, subways, train, and airplane arrivals and departures. These will be useful for many activities in math.

353. Children choose five stocks from the New York Stock Exchange and keep a table of their daily progress.

354. Use the Thursday newspaper for grocery specials. Compare prices of three different stores for the same items. Each "bargain" may be circled. Teams of two to three children may use different stores, or choose differing types of groceries.

ITEM	STORE A	STORE B	STORE C
potatoes	.19 lb.	.12 lb.	.20 lb.
hot dogs	1.19 lb.	1.19 lb.	1.21 lb.
ice cream	.79 qt.	.85 qt.	.59 qt.

IV. SCIENCE AND HEALTH

355. Divide the class into two teams. Each player should have a pencil, paper, and a dictionary. The players divide their papers into three columns, as shown below, and label the columns *food, clothing,* and *shelter.*

The teacher then writes on the chalkboard a list of unfamiliar words that can be definitely categorized, such as *asparagus, cathedral, surplice, succotash, sari, gazebo.*

Students use their dictionaries to determine the correct column in which to write each word. A point is scored for each word correctly placed, and the team with the most points wins the game.

FOOD	CLOTHING	SHELTER

356. Choose topics such as *wood, glass, plastic,* and *metal.* Go around the room, giving each child a turn to name an object made from the material chosen. He may not duplicate something already given. If he is unable to think of a new word, he is "out."

357. A scrambled bulletin board is an excellent way to introduce new vocabulary words to be used in a unit. This may be used with science, social studies units, or language arts areas such as syllables, compound words, rhyming words, antonyms, homonyms, synonyms, prefixes, or suffixes. Write "Scramble Board" diagonally across the board. Each word being used is divided into two sections; place one section on one side of the board, the second on the other side, as in Illustration 357.

Below the board, display items that will be used in the study unit. If it is being used as a language board, pictures or charts with related words may accompany the display.

ILLUSTRATION 357.

EXAMPLES

WORDS USED	ITEMS TO ACCOMPANY BOARD	
aquarium	aquarium	guppies
microscope	pond water	gravel
terrarium	net	microscope
guppies	fish	plants

358. Give each student a dittoed copy of fifteen words and ten sentences. A word has been omitted in each sentence. Students choose the correct word to complete each sentence. There will be five words left over. Vocabulary drawn from science texts is reinforced in this way.

EXAMPLES

plague	circumference	consequence
typhoon	precaution	biology
serene	astronomy	tropical
talons	grotesque	tycoon
illustrations	industrious	duplicate

1. The eagle sank his _____ into the wildcat.

2. The distance around a circle is called its _____.

3. _____ is the study of the heavenly bodies.

4. _____ is the study of animal life.

5. A _____ is a violent storm.

6. The _____ for the book were done by a noted artist.

7. The hunchback of Notre Dame was a _____ figure.

359. Science and health vocabularies are often more difficult than the vocabulary in readers. To reinforce learning of

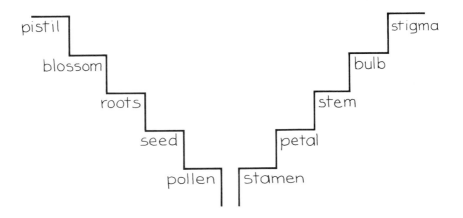

ILLUSTRATION 359.

these new words, try this game. Draw two sets of stairs on the board. On each step write one of the new words (see Illustration 359). The players on two teams (no more than four on a team) take turns pronouncing and giving a meaningful sentence using the word in its proper context for that lesson. One point is scored for each correct answer, and the team with the most points wins.

360. The teacher and students make a chart together listing words coming into common use today. Words invented for commercial purposes, such as acetate or nylon, may also be included.

EXAMPLES

lunar module
mohair
clicks

8

Advanced
Reading Skills

Rationale

Some authors give us long lists of comprehension skills, despite their inability to demonstrate real differences among these skills. There are only three or four components of comprehension recognized by research. One of these, of course, is the difficulty of the vocabulary for the reader. We attempt to increase the reader's vocabulary by training in using word analysis and contextual clues.

A second major component is the recognition of relationships among ideas, as in adding them together to find a main idea, distinguishing among major and minor details, following a sequence of related directions, and adding ideas together to make an inference or draw a conclusion. Most other so-

called comprehension skills are simply extensions of these basic behaviors.

As the pupil progresses to more difficult materials, his organizing skills and rates of reading begin to influence his comprehension. If he is to obtain the breadth and depth of comprehension demanded in later school life, he must learn to summarize and outline, to separate reasonable from exaggerated language, and to vary his reading rate for different reading tasks.

THE CHILD WILL LEARN:

to express the main idea of a given selection

to find and remember various details

to follow sequential directions

to coalesce ideas to draw conclusions

to demonstrate his comprehension in a variety of ways

to manipulate his rate according to his purpose and the difficulty of the material

to prepare simple summaries and outlines

to deal with materials incorporating fact and exaggeration, time and cause-effect relationships

---

I. UNDERSTANDING WHAT IS READ

SELECTING TITLE FOR STORY

361. *Hint:* Always stress the main idea when selecting a title.

362. Read a story to a group. Afterwards, ask the group for suggestions of possible titles for the story. List each reasonable suggestion on the board. Discuss these and the group decides on one or two titles that seem most appropriate.

363. Tape a paper cover over the title of a new book and cover the title on the title page or fasten it to the cover with a paper clip. Leave the book out so it is available to students. Those who read it must write a possible title on the paper cover. Students enjoy reading others' proposed titles.

364. Have students read selected paragraphs and supply three titles for each one. One should be an action title, one a mood title, and one a suspense title.

LOCATING AND REMEMBERING
DETAILS AND FACTS

365. *Hint:* When asking questions concerning details and facts, ask only for interesting or important information. Avoid questions that do not add to the comprehension of the selection.

366. Divide the class into two teams. Each team lines up in a row. The leader reads a spelling word, a sound, or a word containing a sound being studied. This is the signal to begin. The first child on each team must hop, skip, or walk to the board, write the word or words called and return to the end of their line. When both teams' children have returned, the next in line are given their turn. The team writing the most correctly spelled words is the winner.

367. The child who is "It" says to the class, "I am thinking of the name of a country; what is it?" Students then try to guess the country by asking pertinent questions. The one who is "It" can answer only "Yes" or "No." For example, "Is it on the continent of Europe?" "Is it in the southern part of Europe?" "Is it bordered by the Mediterranean Sea?" "Is it Italy?"

The one who guesses correctly the name of the country is then "It," and the game continues with the class asking leading questions about the country, invention, famous person, or other topic he is thinking of.

VARIATION

> *This game may be played by younger children by using rhyming words. The one who is "It" says, "I am thinking of a word that sounds like 'cat,' and it is something to wear." The children then guess what it is, knowing the answer must rhyme with "cat."*

368. Assorted newspaper ads may be used to develop skills in reading comprehension and in locating information. Paste several ads on a piece of paper. On a separate sheet, write questions that can be answered from reading the ads. Let students study the ads and locate information needed to answer the questions. Also make an answer sheet. All three sheets may be kept together in a folder.

VARIATION

> *The Yellow Pages of a telephone directory are excellent sources for ads.*

369. A fun way to check comprehension of an assigned story or study unit is a "Circle Review" game. The group forms a circle, and the first player asks the player on his right a question about the story or unit. If the player answers correctly, he gets a point and is the next person to ask a question. If he is not able to answer correctly, the question continues around the circle until someone answers correctly. The game

continues until each person is given several chances to participate. Individual scores may be kept to see who is the winner.

VARIATION

> *Spelling words may be used instead of questions.*

FOLLOWING DIRECTIONS

370. The child is given a list of words and follows
two sets of directions.

EXAMPLE

 Draw a ring around things you can *wear*. Put two
lines under things you can *do*.

coat	shirt	dress
walk	play	shoes
swim	run	hat

371. Bring an object such as an eraser to the front of
the room, then ask a child to find an object associated with the
eraser. Or ask the child to find a piece of paper larger than the
one you are holding or a book that is larger. This exercise not
only develops visual acuity but helps build vocabulary concepts.

372. This activity may be played indoors or outside.
Mark off an area about four feet wide and ten feet long. Within
this area form an obstacle course by placing objects such as a
trash can, books, a ball, an eraser, crumpled paper, and the like.
One person is blindfolded and tries to walk through the obstacle
course by listening to directions. The person giving directions
tries to guide the player around or over the objects with di-

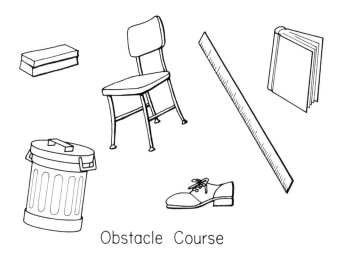

Obstacle Course

ILLUSTRATION 372.

rections like, "Lift your right leg high and step forward about two feet," or "More to the left and go forward." This activity is as much fun for observers as for participants!

373. Pupils should learn to write clear directions as well as to follow them. Instruct pupils to write interesting action directions on strips of stiff paper. Collect the strips and place them in a container of some kind so that students cannot read them before drawing one out. Each student draws a strip and follows the directions on it.

VARIATION

> *If it is near Easter, roll the directions and place them in small plastic eggs that can be opened and closed.*

374. Plan to prepare from a recipe some type of food for students to eat. This, of course, involves following directions closely. Several committees can plan and prepare different dishes.

Raise your right hand and put it down

Say "hello" to a friend.

Hop 3 times on your left foot.

Pick up paper around your desk.

Sharpen your pencil.

ILLUSTRATION 373.

375. On the board or on a chart, print written directions as follows:

1. *Use a ruler to make a large square.*

2. *Within the large square, draw a circle touching the square on all four sides.*

3. *Within the circle, draw another square, touching the circle at four points.*

4. *With crayons, color each area differently: outside the inner square and within the inner circle.*

5. *Within the inner square, draw any shape or shapes you think will fit. Be sure each shape touches the square on at least three sides.*

376. Have students listen to TV and radio announcements that direct listeners to send for free material. Have them copy down the information and check for accuracy.

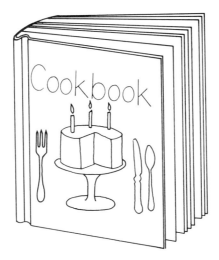

ILLUSTRATION 374.

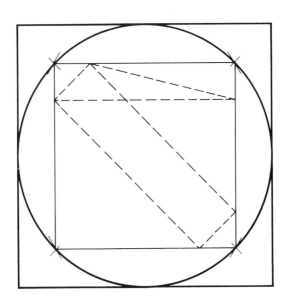

ILLUSTRATION 375.

377. List several sentences on the board. Some sentences should call for listening for comprehension, and some for following written directions. Have students read the sentences and give the correct responses.

EXAMPLES

1. *In the top right-hand corner of your paper, write your name and grade.*

2. *Draw five kittens. Color four brown and one black.*

3. *Draw a circle around the black kitten.*

4. *There are three girls in the front row. Write the name of the girl who has blond hair.*

DRAWING CONCLUSIONS AND
ANTICIPATING OUTCOMES

378. After a basal reader has been read, divide the group into two teams. Ask questions pertaining to the various stories. Alternate from team to team, player to player, scoring *one* point for correct answers, subtracting *five* points for an error.

EXAMPLES

In which story did the waves wash over the

   seawall?

An alligator was in this story.

One story had a song in it.

Which story had a sad ending?

379. Ditto sentences pertaining to eight objects. After each sentence, write a number for the position of the described object (see Illustration 379). Leave a blank space at the top of the paper. Have students read each sentence and draw a descriptive illustration in the given position.

380. Make a spirit master of phrases that tell *who, what, when,* and *how.* To the right of the sentences make a chart, as in Illustration 380. Students check the appropriate response.

381. Use a reading text or other subject matter textbook, and have students locate sentences on a given page that tell how, when, where, why, or who. Write the headings on the board. An oral discussion follows, with each student participating. Give attention to some sentences that will apply to more than one question.

382. Direct each student to read a story about a famous person or an invention, an event in history, or a nation.

1	2	3	4
5	6	7	8

1. It likes milk. __7__	5. You write with it. __1__
2. I have a tail and I fly. __6__	6. You clean the floor with this. __5__
3. You wind it and it runs. __8__	7. It rings. __3__
4. It is alive. __4__	8. It shines at night. __2__

ILLUSTRATION 379.

Phrases	Who	What	When	Where	How
1. on the sunny side				✓	
2. the first grade boy	✓				
3. winds and high water		✓			
4. yesterday at sunrise			✓		
5. turn very slowly					✓
6. through the window				✓	
7. my brother's friend	✓				
8. the yellow school bus		✓			

ILLUSTRATION 380.

Then have the student write down ten clues as to the person's identity. The clues should become progressively more explicit, without revealing the person's name. Select one student to read his first clue, then have the class guess the person's identity. If they are unable to do so with the first clue, have the student read the second, third, and so on, until one student guesses the person's name. The one who guesses correctly then reads his clues, again one clue at a time.

383. While children are reading an unfamiliar story, have them stop at a dramatic or interesting episode. Instruct them to cover the next few lines with paper and try to anticipate what will happen next. Urge the students to use illustrations and text in deciding the probable ensuing action.

II. INTERPRETATION THROUGH SHARING

DRAMATIZATION

384. Have children choose roles and read or dramatize the conversation of characters in a story, stressing the need to "talk like real people," to "show how you feel by your voice," and other such factors.

385. A few students dramatizing scenes from unfamiliar stories may encourage other students to read the stories. The productions may be elaborate, with stage settings and costumes, or they may be simple, with little preparation. The actors may construct their own narration and dialogue, or they may learn excerpts from the author's words.

386. Write on the chalkboard words for emotions, such as happiness, fear, anger, and love. The children dramatize each of them, using various facial expressions, gestures, and tones of voice.

Follow-up: To further develop the ability to portray emotions, have the class dramatize a familiar story. Prepare them by first discussing the plot, character, setting, and the most effective techniques of achieving tone and emotional reaction.

387. Children will enjoy making hand or stick puppet characters taken from a story, for example, the spider from *Charlotte's Web.* The puppets may then be used to dramatize the story for others.

388. Students may use a story from a reader or a library book to simulate a radio play. Give special attention to creating sound effects.

389. For practice in oral reading and communication, pupils may write a radio script using topics, such as "modern

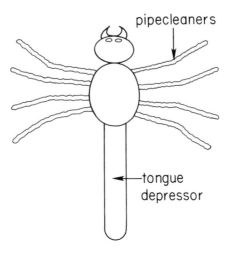

pipecleaners

tongue
depressor

ILLUSTRATION 387.

space travel" or "weather satellites," and produce it on a tape recorder. Advanced students may want to carry this activity a step further by expanding it into a "live television" presentation.

SHARING BOOKS

390.   Flannelboard characters and scenes provide an interesting way of presenting a book. Students may make the figures from felt or draw them on heavy paper. If paper figures are used, glue a small piece of sandpaper, felt, or pellon on the back of each one so it will stick to the flannel. Each child may narrate his own story as he displays the scenes.

391.   The title of a book and its characters may be displayed by using simple mobiles made from clothes hangers.

392.   Book jackets may be displayed on library tables or on bulletin boards. Illustrations and authors are discussed, and children try to find other stories illustrated by the same artist.

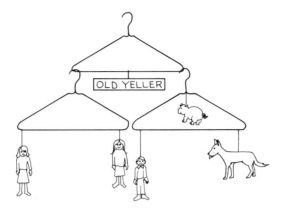

ILLUSTRATION 391.

393. A "bookworm" may be used to keep a list of the books read by each child. Each child cuts circles from colored construction paper and makes one to resemble the worm's head. On assorted colored circles, the child writes the name and author of each book he has read. The circles are overlapped to form the worm, which may be hung up along the wall or used on a bulletin board.

394. Have each student select a library book. Each student may share something about the book, describe the main characters, or read an interesting portion of the book to a small group of volunteer listeners.

395. Students can make small bookcases from cardboard cartons. Cut the box to resemble Illustration 395. Boxes may be painted, covered with contact paper, or decorated in other ways. This is a good way to arrange your library collection into interest areas.

396. Arrange on the bulletin board a series of bordered sheets of paper. Head each paper with a method of reporting; students share their reports at a time set aside for

ILLUSTRATION 395.

sharing books. Students sign the sheets, indicating their choices. Change headings often, as students think of different ways to share books. Examples of headings include puppetry, diorama, character analysis, drawing, skit, written report, mural, book jacket.

397. To share comprehension of a book or story, students make a collage using pictures and words from magazines on a piece of oaktag. If other children in class have read that story, let them tell what the collage is saying.

How Will You Share?

Puppetry	Skit	Written Report
1. _____	1. _____	1. _____
2. _____	2. _____	2. _____
3. _____	3. _____	3. _____
4. _____	4. _____	4. _____
5. _____	5. _____	5. _____
6. _____	6. _____	6. _____
7. _____	7. _____	7. _____
8. _____	8. _____	8. _____
9. _____	9. _____	9. _____
10. _____	10. _____	10. _____
11. _____		11. _____

ILLUSTRATION 396.

ILLUSTRATION 398.

398. A book diorama is an activity which can be undertaken by the class as a group or by individuals. The class (or individual) selects a scene from a book and reconstructs it inside a box from which the top has been removed. The box may be decorated with construction paper, paints, or other materials, and the characters may be made from cardboard or clay.

399. For a different kind of book report, use the format of comic strips. Give each student a long piece of draw-

ILLUSTRATION 399.

ing paper. The child divides it into boxes and fills each box with one scene from a story. The title and author are printed along the top of the strip. The child may write a short summary of the story on the back of the strip.

CHARACTER ANALYSIS

400.   Allow students to perform certain actions described in the text, such as "sauntering about," "swaggering," or "loping along." Urge them to show by their own actions and expressions how the character looked and acted.

401.   Students may use clay to mold characters of a story. These may be used for stimulation in discussing character analysis or in a review of the story.

402.   Give each child a copy of a brief story that contains a spirited dialogue (or refer to a passage in the text). Instruct the class to skim the selection to find descriptive words and phrases that give a more definite description of how the characters felt and sounded. As they find such phrases as "whispered Bill," "he stammered," "agreed Eric," or "David remarked," have students read the passages aloud and describe the character's emotional intent.

Follow-up: As a writing experience, students may compose one-paragraph conversations, substituting descriptions of the way the character spoke for the words he may actually have said.

403.   After reading a story to the class, lead students in a review of the plot and of the characters' responses to each situation. Urge pupils to cite evidence from the story of each character's mood and manner. Then have certain students read the conversations again, capturing the character's reactions by tone and emphasis.

404. To organize information about story characters, students may locate and read aloud the answers to questions such as those below.

Who is the main character?
What does he look like?
Where does he live?
What does he like to do?
How does he act?
Is the character like you in any way?
About how old is this character?

405. After students have read a story, they may write an analysis of a particular character. The sketch may pertain only to information found in the story, or it may include personal impressions of the character which were not described in the story.

406. After the class has read a story, write on the chalkboard words and phrases that describe emotional responses of the characters. Have students name the character who made each response and describe the events in the story that evoked that emotion.

He scowled	Jason
She stammered	Alice
He laughed and laughed	Jason
Tears ran down her cheeks	Mother

III. RATE IMPROVEMENT

SPEED

407. *Hint:* To decrease lip movement while reading silently, let the reader place an object in his mouth, such as a lollypop, pencil, or chewing gum.

408. *Hint:* If you have access to Science Research Associates Reading Kits, the Rate Builders are useful for increasing speed of reading.

409. The teacher prepares in advance groups of letters written on large cards or on a transparency for the overhead projector. Examples of letter groupings are given below. Then divide the class into two teams, and direct all students to have a pencil and paper ready. Then, as the children watch, holding up their pencils, show the letters for about five seconds. Then say "Begin." Each player writes the letters as he remembers them. One point is scored for each group of letters written in the proper sequence. The team with the most points wins.

EXAMPLES

ajm	clpk	vbnih	qwetipl
clo	jril	cfgdr	saduoigtr
wtr	subx	xmkio	mbewtypas
pxd	qdft	lkjeg	poikjhbvc

SKIMMING AND SCANNING

410. Divide the group into two teams. Let each player have a book on his desk. The teacher asks a question that may be answered from the book. Questions may be asked about content, number of capitals, periods, vowels, sentences, and other points on particular pages. The first child who answers the question correctly wins a point for his team, and the team with the most points wins.

Note: This activity could be related to any skill involved in reading. Tailor your questions to fit the particular skills you are stressing.

411. Hint: Explain to the group that skimming is a technique used to look quickly over reading material so that you can decide if it interests you enough to really read the article. Materials we often skim are newspapers, magazines, TV schedules, and menus.

412. Discuss with the class the fact that newspapers are designed for quick and easy reading (skimming). The first sentence of an article usually answers four basic questions: who, what, when, where. The remainder of the article adds the details. Instruct each student to bring a newspaper article to class. Have several students place their articles in an opaque projector. The class determines the answers to the four basic questions about each article.

413. The newspaper is a good source for material to speed up reading. Give a child a page from the paper and ask him to skim the content for about two minutes. When the time is up, have him fold up the page and list on scratch paper the articles he would be interested in reading. Students then exchange pages and repeat the exercise.

This activity is only meant to give students practice in skimming so that they may employ this skill when reading the daily newspaper.

414. Explain to your students that scanning is involved when you know what you are looking for and you are just trying to find it.

A particular name in a telephone book
A TV program in a guide
A certain movie in the newspaper
A time on a subway schedule
A word in the dictionary

415. Instruct the class to read a passage from their science text, finding as quickly as possible the answer to a specific question, such as "Find the names of the two main bones of the arm." Give as much time as needed in the beginning for scanning, but shorten the time as students become more proficient.

416. Upper-grade children enjoy this news activity. Choose five news categories, such as local politics, national

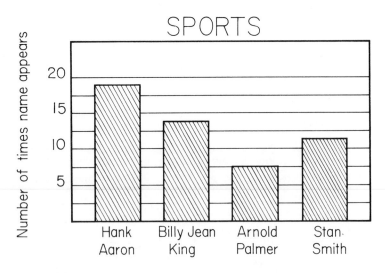

ILLUSTRATION 416.

politics, sports, theater, science. Assign a committee to each category. Each committee chooses several prominent people associated with their category. Daily, for a week, students search through the local newspaper and keep a tally as to the number of times their VIPs' names appear in the news.

    Follow-up: If you are working on bar graphs, this is an opportune time to have each committee make a graph of results.

    417. The reading rates of children may be checked with a small group. Be sure the material is easy to read and of interest to the children. Have them read as fast as they comfortably can, but they should not skim. Give several timed checks in sequence. Ask a variety of questions to check comprehension.

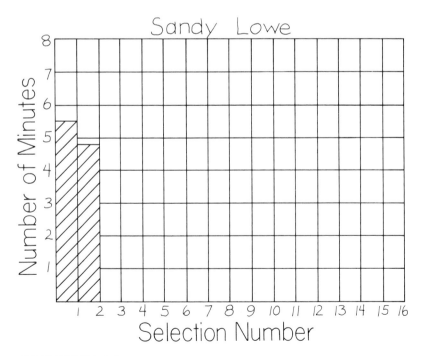

ILLUSTRATION 417.

A rate record may be made as shown in Illustration 417. This activity is not intended for primary grades.

IV. ORGANIZING SKILLS

SEPARATING REASONABLE AND EXAGGERATED LANGUAGE

418.   List several humorous statements, some that are possible to see on earth and some that are exaggerations of reality. Students circle the statements that are exaggerations.

EXAMPLES

an elephant talking
two cars tied together
a boy standing on a man's shoulder
an odd-looking spacecraft
a person weighing 1,200 pounds
a house four stories high
a crocodile twenty feet long

419.   Read "tall tales" to the class, and have children listen for exaggerations and tell how many they can remember. After several tales have been read, such as some of the Paul Bunyan stories, divide the class into groups of five or six students. Let them make up a "tall tale" to share with the class.

420.   Students bring in advertising slogans from magazines, newspapers, or TV commercials. Instruct students to rewrite each slogan in a different style from its original form. For example, if the slogan is written as a play on words, the student can rewrite it as a completely imaginative or as a truthful statement. Or, if the slogan is a straightforward statement, the student could make it a gross exaggeration.

421. Cut advertising slogans from magazines and let pupils analyze them for a language arts lesson. Discuss whether each statement is true, a play on words, exaggerated, or completely imaginative.

EXAMPLES

Put a tiger in your tank *(Exxon).*
You can't eat one *(potato chips).*
When you've got your health, you've got just
about everything *(Geritol).*
The Now generation *(Pepsi).*
The Greatest Show on Earth *(Ringling Brothers*
and Barnum and Bailey Circus).

FINDING IRRELEVANT PARTS,
SORTING RELATED STATEMENTS

422. *Hint:* Tell a simple story to the group. Deliberately include several irrelevant sentences. Ask the students to repeat as many of the irrelevant sentences as they can remember. Later, when you are reading a story to the group, insert a few irrelevant sentences, not changing your tone of voice. See if students are listening and thinking!

423. Give careless readers a paragraph containing various parts that do not fit the meaning of the rest of the paragraph. When the child locates an incorrect or unlikely statement, he crosses it out.
Follow-up: Students can rewrite the paragraph as they believe it should be written.

The Reed family lived in the settlement of Boonesboro. Early one evening Tom and Joe were doing their homework. They were sitting on a stool by the fireplace. The TV was going but they weren't watching. Suddenly the lights went out. Dad went to check and found a fuse had blown out. He replaced it and the electricity came back on. The boys quickly finished their homework and started watching the football game with their father.

424. Pictures of various types of communication devices (radio, TV, tape recorder, microphone, typewriter, record, telephone, Morse code sender) are placed before the group. Each student chooses one device (not telling which he has chosen) and spends several days accumulating information about it. To this information he adds irrelevant information of his choice. When each student presents his information to the group, the other students must decide which device is described and which statements are irrelevant.

ORGANIZATION OF PARAGRAPH—
TOPIC AND SUMMARY SENTENCES

425. Collect materials that can be thrown away, such as newspapers, magazines, or folders. Students circle the topic sentence and underline supporting details. Keep a master copy available for self-checking.

426. Use your basal reader for practice in finding the main idea of a paragraph. Lightly, with pencil, students consecutively number the paragraphs in a story. Then they write the numbers on paper and write a sentence after each number stating the main idea of that paragraph. (It should be noted that not every paragraph has a strong main idea.)

427. Assign students to watch a sketch from their favorite TV variety show. Afterwards they describe the main idea and write several supporting sentences.

428. Write twelve groups of three statements. In each group, write one sentence that states a cause, one an effect, and one that is irrelevant to the other two. Students place a C beside the cause, *E* beside the effect, and *I* beside the irrelevant sentence.

EXAMPLES

The car skidded. (E)
The road was slippery. (C)
The gas was running low. (I)

Chocolate is her favorite ice cream. (I)
She didn't have time for breakfast. (C)
She was hungry all morning. (E)

429. Children mark a piece of paper into columns, as shown below. Then they read an assigned story and list words or phrases that express *time, place, event,* and *cause*. These words should be listed under the correct column headings. This may be done as a small group activity, allowing time for discussion and evaluation.

TIME	PLACE	EVENT	CAUSE
late afternoon	Orchard Road	accident	rain

430. To make community history more meaningful and interesting, let students interview older members of the community to learn facts concerning its early settlement, industry, homes, and development. Invite members of the community to the classroom as resource visitors. The class may write articles or stories based on the information learned.

Follow-up: Students can make a display showing how the community has changed through the years, with an accompanying folder explaining the causes of the changes.

SEQUENCE OF EVENTS

431. Children may compare several pictures, including one that does not belong in the series. They are asked to find the one that does not belong. Loose pictures, comic books, or comic strips may be used effectively.

432. After a field trip, students make a display chart showing the sequence of events. The display may include illustrations.

433. Use either a commercial ring-toss peg or make one from the core of a roll of paper. Write a story on rings of stiff oaktag, one sentence per ring. Students place the rings on the peg in sequential order.

434. Three different stories are cut into separate paragraphs. Mount each paragraph on an index card. Students must determine which paragraphs go with each story. Next, they arrange the paragraphs in sequence. Old basal readers are perfect for this activity.

For self-checking, place the correct number of the paragraph in its sequence on the reverse side of each card. Keep the cards in an envelope so that they do not become mixed with other activities. This is a useful activity for a learning station.

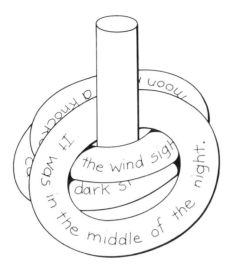

ILLUSTRATION 433.

435. Read a story to the class, then cite a particular incident from it. Have students describe what happened just before and just after the incident. Then direct the class's attention to a particular illustration in the story, and have them describe what event the illustration refers to, what action preceded it, and what followed.

436. Placing story events in sequence can be a difficult task for some students. Begin with only three sentences in mixed order, then increase the number as students become more capable. Use simple stories that contain useful information.

EXAMPLES

A GOOD STORY

(2) read the book
(1) open the book
(3) put the book away

MAKE THAT CALL

_____ dial number
_____ wait for an answer
_____ listen for dial tone
_____ lift receiver

437. This activity is especially important when students are learning to write their own stories. To develop awareness of the sequence of events in a story, have the class review such phrases as *to begin with, then, following, next, after that,* and *in conclusion.* Instruct students to examine the story for words and phrases that indicate time, such as when an event took place or how long something lasted.

438. A recorded story, news event, or short talk is presented to the class. Have the students write the main events in correct sequence as they occurred in the talk. Reread or replay the record so students may check their skill.

WRITING BRIEF SUMMARIES

439. *Hint:* Western Union will supply you with telegram blanks. Use them for practice in condensing information in the simplest form. Telegrams may be written or typed in appropriate style. Western Union will also give you old telegrams as samples.

OUTLINING

440. To share reading experiences, children may make bulletin board book reviews. After the student has read a book, he writes on a 3 × 5 card such information as title, author, setting, a one- or two-sentence summary of the plot, and a brief explanation of why he liked the book. The cards are tacked to the bulletin board for others to read.

VARIATION

> *File the cards in a file box to be kept on the library table.*

441. The class or group is divided into two or more teams. Each pupil is given an interesting magazine picture or diagram, a pencil, and a piece of paper. Each child writes a sentence caption for his picture. If his caption is a sentence and it expresses the main idea of the picture, the child receives a point. The team with the most points is the winner. The object of the game is to help pupils learn to form a good summary sentence. For this reason, points are allowed only for complete sentences. Be sure to point out that phrases may also summarize ideas.

442. To personalize outlining skills, instruct students on how to make an outline of their own personal daily schedule.

EXAMPLE

My School Day
  I. *Pre-School Morning Activities*
     A. *Home*
        1.
        2.
        3.
     B. *On arrival at school*
        1.
        2.
        3.
 II. *"After the bell rings" activities*
     A.
     B.
        1.
        2.

9

Extra
Added
Attractions

In a collection of activities such as this book, some ideas do not seem to fit into any particular skill area. These include activities for special holidays, seasons, codes, and the like.

444. *Hint:* Blank playing cards with a plastic finish are excellent for making your own card games. You can mark on them and make many kinds of games. They are shipped only in boxes of a thousand, and a minimum order is required, so you will need to "talk it up" with your fellow teachers. The cards are available from Atlantic Playing Card and Match Company, 1005 Thirty-fifth Avenue, Long Island City, New York 11106.

445. The class may wish to make a news board to be situated outside their room. They may post room news, school

NEWS
Last night the
A and P Store had
a big fire. Joe's
daddy works
there.

ILLUSTRATION 445.

news, community information, or important events from news-papers (moon launch, opening of shopping center) for all to enjoy.

446. One section of the board can be set aside for sharing classroom news. Children who have something to share may write it on paper, discuss needed corrections with the teacher, then write the news on the board. At the end of the day the news is read aloud. As a penmanship lesson, the news is written on paper to go in a binder labeled *Class News*. A booklet may be kept for the entire year to relate important class news.

447. *Hint:* If you are using a basal reading book containing unrelated stories, it is not necessary to read the stories in sequence. You may stimulate interest by letting the group select the next story to be read.

448.   Ask the children to write a paragraph without using one letter of the alphabet. Have each child exchange paragraphs with the child sitting next to him. Then each tries to find out what the missing letter is.

EXAMPLE

Painting can be fun. Creating a variety of colors that are pleasing to the eye is a rewarding and satisfying experience. Almost everyone likes pretty colors. The zoo is a nice place to go to paint a picture. It is quiet and peaceful, has interesting animals, pretty trees, and grass. (J is missing.)

449.   Holding the hooked part of a wire coathanger away from you, take hold of each outer edge of the hanger and bend them downward, causing the wire to bow up (see Illustration 449). Bend the hook down, using it as a back rest for a bookstand. This may be used as a stand for reference books, for typing material, or as a display for posters, children's art work, or pictures.

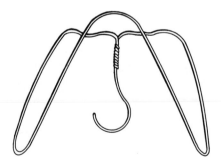

ILLUSTRATION 449.

450. *Hint:* Keep a piece of newsprint handy and use it to blot someone's painting. After using it this way several times, the newsprint will look like an abstract painting.

Suggestion: Ask children to write a brief paragraph describing what they see in the picture.

451. The student who begins this game states that he is thinking of something the class has studied in a particular area or in a book he has read. He then gives one leading statement about the person, event, or story he is thinking of, such as "I am thinking of an American writer of the nineteenth century." The class tries to read his mind; if they fail, he adds another statement as a clue, as, "This writer's best-known book deals with two boys' adventures in a town on the Mississippi." The questions and clues continue until someone guesses correctly. This child then becomes the leader for the next round of the game.

452. After a story or book has been read, a discussion may follow to call attention to materials mentioned in the story. Students may then describe or make objects they can construct from the materials mentioned.

EXAMPLE

If a *box* is mentioned in the story, some of these ideas may be suggested:

cart	table
bookcase	stool
toy chest	flower planter

453. To check the frequent usage of basic sight words, such as *it, this, that, is, was, I, the,* and *you,* have students carefully check their library book or even a single story. By counting these words as they appear, a tally may be kept to determine the frequency of word usage. The count may be kept as a weekly tally for the class or a small group. A chart may also be made to record the data. This type of activity can also serve as an introduction to percentages and averages in graphs and tables.

			Word Frequency		
name	it	this	that	is	the
Susan	7	8	5	11	10
Bill	8	4	3	7	4
Ted	3	6	2	6	12
Debbie	9	5	9	6	9
	27	23	19	30	37
Averages:	6.75	5.75	4.75	7.5	8.75

454. Rule a large sheet of plastic or oilcloth into thirty squares. Write (in cursive or manuscript) a different letter in twenty-six of the squares, and make a star in each of the remaining four squares. Then make a dozen or so small (about

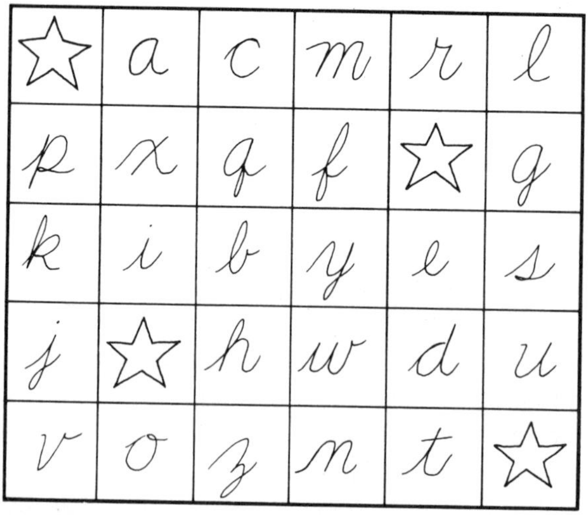

ILLUSTRATION 454.

2 × 2) cards for each letter of the alphabet, but make fewer for *q, v, w,* and make more for *a, e, i, o.* Lay these cards in alphabetical order for easy distribution.

Standing about ten feet from the mat, a child throws a sponge, beanbag, or eraser onto the mat. He receives a matching letter card from a child acting as "supervisor." The player accumulates letters and makes as many words as he can, writing them on his paper while others have a turn. If he lands on a star, he may have a letter of his choice. The winner is the child with the most words when playing stops.

455. A group of students selects (or is assigned) a story with vivid auditory images. Instruct the group to tell the story using only sound effects to relate the action. Narrative may be read, while students perform the sounds, but leave out words or phrases that are "sounded."

456. *Hint:* Inexpensive windowshades make an excellent base for hanging charts that need to be used year after

ILLUSTRATION 456.

year. If you can, get some from Goodwill Industries inexpen-
sively. These shades are also good to cut and use as mats and
gameboards for many activities. Marking pens work well on the
durable surface, and the material can be folded for easy storage
in envelopes.

457. When introducing intermediate-level students
to the geometrical terms like *quadrilateral, parallelogram,* or
trapezoid, show them Illustration 457. Then they make their own
designs with colored papers, using the shapes. This project takes
considerable skill in measuring, and should not be hurried. Some
students need several days for completion of their designs. The
finished products make interesting bulletin board displays.

458. Using an exercise or story already on the board,
dismiss the children by having them locate given things in the
sentences. You may let them find the part asked for, erase it, and
line up at the door for play period, lunch, or class dismissal.

EXAMPLES

Find a compound word.
Find a root word with a prefix.
Find a four-syllable word.
Find a word with a silent letter.
Erase all the capital letters.
Find a word that can be abbreviated.

459. Have students make their own personal book-
marks for each subject area. Cut squares out of oaktag and fold
them into triangles. Staple the sides and cut along fold. Decorate
each according to the subject area.

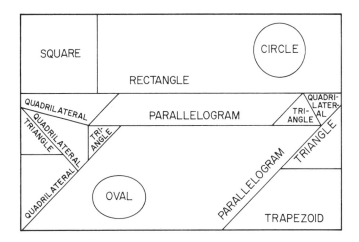

460. Construct a "private office" for students to retreat into when they feel the need to withdraw into quietness. A large box used for shipping mattresses, refrigerators, or washing machines is perfect. Arrange the box like a study carrel. You may need to cut one side out. Inside, place large pillows, a rocking chair, a desk—anything to make it comfortable. You will probably find you need three of them, as they will be very popular.

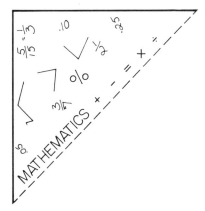

ILLUSTRATION 459.

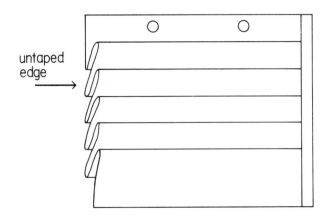

untaped
edge
→

ILLUSTRATION 461.

461. *Hint:* A handy card holder may be made from a piece of large posterboard or oaktag. If oaktag is used, the rows may be made by pleating the paper accordion-style, then stapling the edges. The edges may be trimmed with colored tape. If posterboard is used, make the rows by cutting strips of paper and taping them in place with colored tape. The strips may be cut from the same colored poster board to make a neat appearance. This apparatus may be used for vocabulary practice or as an independent activity, having the child form sentences from experience stories. A smaller version of this activity may be used at students' desks for any variety of practice purposes. Card holders can also be made from accordion-pleated paper.

462. Rip stories from old readers and bind them to make reading booklets. A different colored cover may be used to designate each level. Comprehension question cards may be inserted in the inside covers. Pictures mounted on the front of each booklet add interest. These booklets are especially useful in science and social studies, when students may need easier reading material than the grade-level text.

463. Book covers often create interest in a book by their colors, or by the designs, moods, or adventures they depict. Students can show their interest in books by making creative book jackets. Remember, a book jacket tells three major things: the title, the author, and an interesting picture about the story. Later, students may want to write their own stories to staple inside the jackets. These books may be played on the reading table for all the class to enjoy.

464. Write a word vertically—one letter beneath another. On the left side of a page, the word is written correctly; on the right, the spelling is backward. Children enjoy using their own names in this way.

Instruct the children to think of words beginning and ending with the letters opposite each other, and to write the words between the letters. For example, the first word might be *guess* or *guppies*. With capable students you might set a five-letter minimum for each word. Students can share lists to increase vocabulary.

465. *Rule of thumb.* Children often have difficulty choosing a book that is on a suitable reading level. Prepare and display a chart with the following directions:

1. *Choose a book that interests you.*

2. *Turn to page 5. Read it.*

3. *Hold up a finger for every word you don't know. If you must use your thumb (for five unknown words), the book may be hard for you.*

4. *If you have to use four fingers or less, try several pages in different parts of the book.*

5. *If you do not use your thumb on more than one page, CHECK IT OUT!*

466. A chart may be kept on the chalkboard or bulletin board to list children appointed as class helpers for each week. Cut a hand from oaktag or construction paper for each child. Print each child's name on a hand. List the duties on the board and as a child assumes responsibility for the job, place his "helping hand" on the chart.

VARIATION

> *Write the duty on the hand, and, as a child is chosen to do the job, print his name on one finger of the hand. In this way the teacher may keep a record so all children will have a turn to perform the duty during the year.*

467. Ask students to think of words that begin and end with the same letter.

EXAMPLES

Moves a football.   __ic__ (kick)
A young dog.   __u__ (pup)
Sloppy eaters need one.   __i__ (bib)
Part of a lamp.   __ul__ (bulb)
Makes a loud noise.   __om__ (bomb)
Shows what you have learned.   __es__ (test)

468. A new simple way to make a flannel board: Cut a rectangular sheet (about 15 × 18 inches) of heavy cardboard. Sew a flannel cover for it just as you would make a pillowcase. That's all there is to it!

469. A quick game while waiting in line. The first person says a word like *blue*. The next person adds a word: *bluebird*. The next *bird cage, cage* _____. If he cannot add a meaningful word, the next person starts with a new word.

470. Make tachistoscopes to reinforce holiday vocabulary. Staple two copies of the shape together so that the vocabulary list can be pulled through (see Illustration 470).

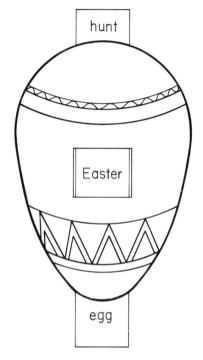

ILLUSTRATION 470.

ILLUSTRATION 471.

ILLUSTRATION 472.

471. Students make large displays before a holiday to emphasize holiday vocabulary. Vocabulary words are attached to the basic figure, as in Illustration 471.

472. Each child makes a cut-out of a holiday figure, such as an egg, Christmas tree, or turkey, and writes an appropriate message down the center. Fellow students' names are written on the figure to mesh with the message, as in Illustration 472. For correct spelling, post a list of names on the bulletin board.

Cross-Index
of Activities

Skill Area	Activity Number
Abbreviations	284, 285, 286, 458
Accent	154, 155
Almanac	291, 292, 293, 294, 295 ,296, 298, 347
Alphabetizing	91, 127, 224, 260, 261, 262, 263, 264, 265, 266, 267, 268, 269, 306, 454
Antonyms	162, 241, 242, 243, 357
Auditory Skills	46, 47, 48, 49, 50, 51, 52, 53, 54, 55, 95, 123, 135, 136, 253, 376, 455
Blending	124, 125, 126, 127, 128, 129
Card Catalog	287, 288, 289
Cause and Effect	412, 428, 429, 430
Classification: Categorizing Words	102, 109, 116, 144, 186, 221, 222, 223, 224, 225, 226, 227, 229, 230, 231, 232, 233, 259, 266, 267, 345, 355, 356
Character Analysis	382, 400, 401, 402, 403, 404, 405, 406
Codes	115, 264, 283, 310
Compound Words	149, 150, 151, 152, 153, 458
Color Discrimination	42, 43, 44, 45, 47
Consonant Blends	106, 107, 127, 138, 170
Consonant Digraphs	105, 109, 127, 138
Contextual Analysis and Clues	67, 79, 103, 129, 131, 146, 154, 155, 187, 188, 189, 190, 191, 192, 193, 194, 195, 258

Skill Area	Activity Number
Index	292, 296
Initial Sounds	47, 54, 91, 95, 96, 97, 98, 99, 100, 101, 102, 103, 108, 136, 137, 138, 170, 190, 467, 469
Interpretation and Dramatization	205, 208, 209, 210, 211, 213, 214, 384, 385, 386, 388, 389, 396, 403, 418, 455
Letter Recognition	4, 39, 40, 41, 62, 63, 64, 101, 454
Map and Globe Skills	315, 319, 320, 321, 322, 323, 324, 325, 326, 327, 328, 329, 330, 331, 332, 333, 334, 335, 336, 337, 338
Main Idea	361, 362, 363, 364, 425, 427
Newspaper	121, 199, 300, 302, 337, 346, 350, 354, 368, 411, 412, 413, 414, 420, 425, 445, 446
Oral Communication	52, 57, 74, 147, 148, 202, 203, 204, 205, 206, 207, 208, 209, 210, 211, 213, 214, 216, 218, 219, 302, 384, 385, 389, 394
Outlining	440, 441, 442
Phonograms	138, 142, 143
Plurals, Inflectional Endings	83, 158, 159, 160, 174, 175, 176, 177, 178, 179
Proverbs	200, 201
Rate Improvement	407, 408, 409, 410, 411, 412, 413, 414, 415, 416, 417

Skill Area	Activity Number
Reference Materials	98, 144, 238, 239, 240, 291, 292, 293, 294, 295, 296, 297, 298, 299, 301, 302, 303, 304, 305, 316, 318, 348, 414, 424, 430
Rhyming Words	135, 139, 140, 141, 142, 143, 144, 367
Root Words, Prefixes, Suffixes	83, 161, 162, 163, 164, 165, 166, 167, 168, 169, 170, 171, 172, 173, 357
Science and Health	172, 280, 301, 355, 356, 357, 358, 359, 360, 374, 415, 462
Sentence Structure	196, 197, 439, 445, 446
Sequence of Events	71, 75, 94, 431, 432, 433, 434, 435, 436, 437, 438, 445, 446
Sharing Books	86, 87, 387, 388, 390, 391, 392, 393, 394, 395, 396, 397, 398, 399, 449, 463
Silent Letters	118, 119, 120, 121, 122, 123, 458
Summarizing	87, 399, 439, 440, 441, 445
Syllabication	125, 180, 181, 182, 183, 184, 185, 186, 458
Synonyms	238, 239, 240, 242
Tables	335, 336, 346, 347, 348, 349, 350, 351, 352, 353, 354, 414, 453
Tactile Discrimination	40, 41, 56, 57, 58, 59, 60, 61, 259
Telephone Directory	269, 270, 271, 306, 307, 308, 309, 310, 311, 312, 313, 314, 315, 316, 317, 318
Topic and Summary Sentences	361, 362, 363, 364, 425, 426, 427, 441